A MEMOIR OF ZERAH COLBURN • ZERAH

Publisher's Note

The book descriptions we ask booksellers to display prominently warn that this is an historic book with numerous typos, missing text or index and is not illustrated.

We scanned this book using character recognition software that includes an automated spell check. Our software is 99 percent accurate if the book is in good condition. However, we do understand that even less than one percent can be a very annoying number of typos! And sometimes all or part of a page is missing from our copy of a book. Or the paper may be so discolored from age that you can no longer read the type. Please accept our sincere apologies.

After we re-typeset and design a book, the page numbers change so the old index and table of contents no longer work. Therefore, we usually remove them.

Our books sell so few copies that you would have to pay hundreds of dollars to cover the cost of proof reading and fixing the typos, missing text and index. Therefore, whenever possible, we let our customers download a free copy of the original typo-free scanned book. Simply enter the barcode number from the back cover of the paperback in the Free Book form at www.general-books. net. You may also qualify for a free trial membership in our book club to download up to four books for free. Simply enter the barcode number from the back cover onto the membership form on the same page. The book club entitles you to select from more than a million books at no additional charge. Simply enter the title or subject onto the search form to find the books.

If you have any questions, could you please be so kind as to consult our Frequently Asked Questions page at www. general-books.net/faqs.cfm? You are also welcome to contact us there.
General Books LLC™, Memphis, USA, 2012. ISBN: 9781151291851.

-:- -:- -:- -:- -:- -:- -:- -:-

nearly three years, was of this desc tion: within its walls, in a large ro nearly a hundred feet long, were tween two and three hundred students, some not more than eight, and some eighteen or nineteen years old, under the care of eight instructers. One branch of Latin study, which we believe is not attended to in our Academies, was taught there, viz. the composition of verse according to the rules of Prosody. The scholar was first directed to make nonsense varses by selecting from a page in Ovid, words of the metre requisite to fill up Hexameter or Pentameter lines. After a week's exercise on this, a selected portion of English, generally out of the Bible, was given, to be rendered into Latin verse.

It is related in the annals of the school, that a celebrated poet, we believe Dryden, while a boy, was a member of the versifying class, when the miracle at Cana of Galilee was given for a subject. The next day the scholars handed in their performances. After commenting upon their merits, the master called on Dryden for his; he replied that he had not done much: he had not been able to get more than one idea, that was appropriate. After chiding him pretty smartly for his indolence, the master called on him to present that one. He came forward, and handed in a piece of paper on which was written,

Lympha pudica Deum vidit, et erubuiu translated thus:

The modest water saw its God, and blushed.

It is needless to add that the delicacy of sentiment, and beautiful fitness of expression, drew from the teacher sudden and large encomiums upon the youthful poet.

While it is easily inferred, from the length of time spent in these seminaries, that erudite scholars would be sent forth, it is but just to state that there are two things in the sanction of these schools, if not matters of requirement, that reflect great dishonor upon their in-

to arms, but to fisticuffs. Such combats frequently occur, and in some cases last one or two hours. Some combatants have had an arm broken, or been otherwise disabled, so as to be hindered for days or weeks from attending to their studies, and all this without eliciting the slightest reproof from their teachers, who being uniformly brought up in the same seminary, either did. not wish to depart from ancient usage, or feared to offend the parents by interfering in these affairs of honor.

The other custom alluded to is a system of servile offices rendered to the members of the Upper school, by the boys in the Lower school; such as cleaning boots and shoesf Candlesticks, washing dishes, brushing clothes, going on errands, &c. &c. This system is denominated *Fagging*. At school with the writer, were sons of the Duke of Bedford, the Marquis of Anglesea, and many other noblemen and gentlemen of high standing, who were not more favored on account of their birth, than the sons of plebians. As might be expected, the master was permitted to inflict such manual castigation upon his Fag, as caprice or cruelty dictated. These schools, sustaining the highest reputation in the kingdom, are well attended; and he that has good talents, nimble fists, and applies to his books, will succeed in obtaining Academic honors. After a course of study in these preparatory seminaries, the way is open for the aspirant after Collegiate distinctions. The establishments at Oxford and Cambridge are in all respects well adapted to nourish and perpetuate the habits acquired by the youthful scholar. He that is of a studious turn and possesses the means, may pass his years at college in completing an education that will prepare him for taking his place among the sons of science and learning in any part of the world; while he that loves company, dissipation and idleness better than his books, may spend his time and his money in such a manner that when leaving the University, he will possess few if any qualifications to secure the esteem of the virtuous and discerning. Yet he is now prepared to be a candidate for promotion in the Army, the Navy, and even, (if he has influential friends) to look for such emoluments as the established church has within its gift.

The Ministers of the Episcopal establishment are in their religious feelings and practice, their morality and talents, very diverse. There are some who, feeling that they are moved by the Holy Ghost to preach, devote their all to the support of the cayse of Truth. Their efforts in this work reflect honor upon their names, while their salutary and reforming influence is felt to the farthest extent of their institution. The number of such men appears to increase; and while united in spirit with those of different sects, who pray, and labor, and suffer for Zion's peace, it may be hoped that amid the political convulsions which agitate the nation, the church of God may yet be safe. Still it is sad and humiliating to remember, that all the stories which we have heard of the fox-hunting, card-playing, drinking, dancing Parson, are not fictitious.

When we look upon the Ecclesiastical hierarchy of England, as it existed without any sensible check; in its full pride and influence, until recently, and while we blame the unnatural union between Church and State as directly leading to the subversion of general evangelical piety, we are liable to forget the circumstances under which, at the period of the Reformation, the Protestant cause arose. We have great reason to adore the guiding hand of a superintending and gracious Providence, which in a day of such moral darkness and ignorance, led the devout inquirer after 5 Truth to contemplate so much light as was then shed forth.

While the principles of the Reformers led them to renounce the supremacy of the Pope, and the mummery of his worship, they were not, in their inexperience, led to see the evil consequences, which under its improved form, still resulted from the connexion between the Civil and the Religious establishments of their age. The progress of reform and improvement has been slow, compared with the wants of mankind, but it has been sure; and at this period we, as citizens of the world, may rejoice in its progress, while as Americans we may likewise exult that it has been reserved for the history of our country, to show how freedom and diversity of sentiment on the subject of religion, may consist with fervent piety, genuine patriotism, and the acceptable discharge of the duties of life.

From the force of early habit, and the intimacies of his youth, the writer has ever been disposed to feel kindly towards a Church, from which John Wesley did not deem it essential to separate himself.

The English as a people freely patronize the arts and sciences: poets, historians, painters, novel-writers and dramatic authors, generally receive, if not all the pecuniary compensation, yet at least all the fame, their works deserve. Improvements in useful knowledge find ready supporters, while aught that can gratify the excited curiosity is sure to prosper. The abundant honor bestowed upon our departed countryman, Benjamin West, is gratifying to American feeling. Another painter, Leslie, was a successful candidate for English popularity nine years ago. It was at the commencement of the last war that Zerah Colburn went to England, and it is but due to their government and people to say that he received as unequivocal marks of kindness and respect as he could have done, if he had been a British subject. Indeed, his situation, as it regarded the patronage of others, was such as would appear enviable to many who are ignorant of the privations which he and his father underwent.

The period which they spent in Europe was one that may be considered a most important one to many of the nations. Then Napoleon was returning from the Russian Campaign, weakened in his power, and already frowned upon by his evil destiny. Unhappy France, for so many years a literal field of blood, after receiving from a foreign power her hereditary Sovereign, and enjoying a brief repose, was doomed to see her Corsican lord return from banishment, and purchase for a hundred days his throne resumed, by the slaughter of thousands of her sons, and husbands, and fathers, at Waterloo. It was during this period, too, that the Prince designed by Nature and Education to sway the British sceptre with glory equal, if not superior to any of his predecessors, after waging ignoble war with the consort of his bed and kingdom for years, sullied the brightness of victory which his arms had gained, and of peace his councils had secured, by dooming the fallen Chief who appeaTed to his generosity for terms, to linger out the remnant of his days upon the barren rocks of St. Helena.

It was in the same length of time also, that our beloved country, roused up to action, confirmed her title to respect and veneration among the governments of the earth, by showing, that having drawn the sword to vindicate her rights, she could sheathe the sword, and practice arts of peace, when those rights were secured. While engaged in the war upon the continent of Europe, England received the news of any victory achieved by her favorite leader, Wellington, with most enthusiastic joy. In addition to the festivities held by princes and nobles in their palaces, the common people expressed their gratulation in a conspicuous manner. Few person's have an idea of the effect produced in the darkness of night by placing a lighted candle against each pane of glass in every window of every house in a town, where for miles each way houses were piled together in close array; while the busy multitudes, forgetting sleep, with songa and shouts and rude mirth, or with more decent, silent pace, were passing from street to street to meet their fellows and exult with them. Large transparent paintings, some allegorical, and some caricatures, were suspended before many of the windows, illustrative of British valor and foreign subjugation. Squibs and crackers were continually snapping, and by their explosion made incessant clashing, while fire works on a larger scale were performed for the amusement of the great.

The English mob would not only rejoice themselves, but they would also compel the inmates of a house not illuminated to light-up, on pain of having every window demolished. This spirit of the populace gave little offence, except to the society of Friends, whose pacific sentiments rendered them opposed to the slaughter of war, by which such victories were gained; but they generally deemed it proper to comply with the excited feelings of the crowd, rather than expose their houses to violence. These occasions of illumination usually continued two or three nights. We do not recollect that London was thus in a blaze on account of any defeat of American arms. *4*

Owing to the want of general information diffused among the people, as well as the great distance between the two countries, the large mass of their population had little or no knowledge of America: they knew that war was carried on, and concluded that success would attend the arms of their country: they expected as a matter of course that King George would do the thing that was right; that the insignificant and undisciplined inhabitants of the States

It is a standing maxim in their government that the King cannot do wrong. would be subdued, and receive their just deserts. Not a few indeed, whose exalted station gave them an ample opportunity of knowing, seemed to be infatuated by a similar delusion. They were not willing to know with how much greater fortitude and perseverance, those could act and suffer, who fought for their country, their families and their homes, than those who, being the hired satellites of an oppressor, have no dearer object than money, promotion, and fame.

The Prince of Wales, who on account of his father's insanity, had been appointed Regent of the kingdom, was in his youth esteemed one of the most promising princes that had ever graced the English history. Led astray by evil examples, taking sides with the impure propensities of nature, and the surrounding temptations which in all their fascinating power courted royal indulgence, he blasted the fair promise of earlier years by a course of luxurious dissipation and folly unknown since the days of Charles the Second. Endowed with a strong constitution, he withstood the power of diseases brought on by Intemperance, for more than forty years. His treatment of his wife, Queen Caroline, before and after her voluntary exile in the different countries of Europe, excited against him a large share of popular indignation; yet in his intercourse with other Potentates, he exhibited talents that commanded respect. His only legitimate child, the Princess Charlotte, heiress apparent to the crown, was endowed by Nature with talents that endeared her to the English, who anticipated days of feculiar prosperity in her reign. Married in early ife to Leopold of Saxe-Cobourg, the illustrious pair seemed not more qualified to command veneration and love in their public capacity, than by exhibiting the harmony and loveliness of conjugal life in its most beautiful form. But the premature death of the Princess in 1817, blasted all those hopes, and wrapt a nation in sorrow and gloom. In their mourning there were many, who, unreconciled to her death, formed an opinion that she and her offspring would have lived, had not authorized cruelty seized that opportunity to destroy her life. Her attending physician a short time afterwards was found dead at his residence. Common report attributed his death to suicide; while some supposed that he was murdered, lest his lips should at some future day publish truths derogatory from the royal character.

The domestic establishments of the Nobility are costly and magnificent. Besides a residence in town, they have one or more country-houses, in which they spend the summer-months, repairing to them during the recess of Parliament. Their wealth is derived, in most instances, from the rents of lands occupied by numerous tenants; and according to their means, their equipages, pomp and state, are conspicuously displayed. With our republican notions, we should think it somewhat strange, if on going to see another on important business, we should be obliged to wait until a troop of servants had consulted on the expediency of carrying in our message to their Lord; the instance seldom if ever occurs that an audience can be obtained without such a preliminary course: and after all, perhaps the waiting applicant is told his Lordship is not disposed to see him. This is frequently the case; and doubly unpleasant, if the visitor should happen to be a suffering, impatient creditor, and find his extravagant, gambling debtor, tinctured with the idea that it is dishonorable for a man of fashion to pay his just debts.

It is customary for Noblemen to retain among their dependants one or more Clergymen in the capacity of Chaplains. This office is for the most part nominal, as it regards any clerical services discharged by them in the families of their patrons, but it furnishes those landholders, whose possessions embrace one or more parishes, with an opportunity of making a handsome provision for a gentleman of parts and learning who has received ordination, and to do it in a way that reminds of dependance, less perhaps than any other in which a kindness might be conferred. A tutor fbr their children is also requisite. The temporal and financial concerns of the household are under the superintendance of the Steward, whose office consequently is first in point of respectability and trust. A coachman to drive his carriage, 'two, three, or four footmen for waiters, and female servants, compose the general number of a nobleman's retinue.

The employments of the great, unless they take an active part in the political interests of the nation, are various. Some devote their time and money to the promotion of literature and science; quite a number are engaged in advancing the cause of religion and benevolence: the army and the navy are served by some, and many spend their substance like the prodigal of old. Their style of living is splendid and luxurious; to our plain manners it furnishes a great-contrast. After a breakfast taken at some hour between eight and twelve o'clock, A. M., the time is passed until five, six, seven or eight o'clock in the afternoon, according to their rank and degree, with a brief repast by way of luncheon in tb« interval; when they surround the table, groaning beneath the luxurious burden of soups, fish, flesh, fowl, venison, pastry, and wine: after active exercise with knife, fork and spoon, during one or two hours, the cloth is removed, the ladies retire to the drawingroom, and the gentlemen remain behind to partake of the dessert, consisting of the choicest fruits, native and foreign; this, with the usual addresses to Port, Madeira, Claret, &c. &c. and the discussion of such topics as present themselves to their inspiration, occupies an hour or two more. Then they join the ladies, drink their tea, and unless further festivities require their presence, when fashion gives permission they retire to rest. The last party at which it wae the author's fortune to be a guest, separated after midnight, when he was taken by his accompanying friends to another place of rendezvous, where a splendid rout was kept up till about five o'clock, when he returned home.

The habits of the common people are very different; their hours of labor, eating and rest, are similar to ours; their diet, simple and healthy. Accordingly the mass of the population is healthy. Residing, at different periods, nearly nine years in the city of London, the author gives it as his opinion, that though in such a vast concourse of inhabitants, some will be sick, and some will die, yet they enjoy a greater immunity from disease than we could reasonably expect.

The country is, generally speaking, level, the roads are uniformly good, and the farms in a high state of cultivation. This seems indispensably requisite, from the fact that so many millions of inhabitants are supported on a tract of land as small as the British Island. Indeed it is very evident that our agriculturalists, as a. general thing, have not discovered the art of subsisting with less labor and less travel, on a small estate, even in a better manner, than while possessing and partially cultivating two, three, or four hundred acres. True, it may be said that land is cheap and our continent immense. But in an age of invention and improvement, like the present, when so mighty an impulse has been given to the energies of the human mind, it is manifest that a science of such vast importance to all ranks and classes, as agriculture, ought, by all lovers of their country, to be pushed to its greatest possible perfection.

In England, he that owns his farm may live.well and provide for his family; the tenant is more embarrassed, and the daily laborer may think himself well off, if by any means, he can secure a scanty pittance for his wife and children. This must always be the case where provisions are high, and the price of labor low.

Some idea of the expensiveness of a city residence may be gathered from the following statement: The annual taxes on a house rented at a hundred and fifty dollars, will be about fifty dollars more. This tbe tenant must pay. But in the city, perhaps no house could be hired at so low a rate, unless in some mean and poor neighborhood: the price of the different kinds of fresh meat per lb. varies from seven to fourteen pence sterling; butter from twelve to twenty four; tea from eight to twenty five shillings; sugar from ten to fourteen pence. All other provisions are proportionably high. On account of the vast competition which prevails among the different trades and mechanical arts, many are obliged to work at the lowest rate; and it is not strange if the avails thereof be found insufficient to support a numerous family in a comfortable style. Seven years' apprenticeship is required by law, before the practice of any mechanical trade: by this regulation, at least one good object is secured, the customer may depend on having his order executed in a proper manner.

The Jewish family are very numerous in London; here, as in other nations where they have gained a residence, they remain a distinct people, fully answering the prophetic description of them in the Scriptures. Distinctly known from Christians by a peculiar expression of countenance, they are equally so by their internal regulations as a community. There are no beggars among them: all who are able to work, are engaged in some calling to provide for themselves; at the same time, they are so generally reputed to be knaves and sharpers, that the English would deem it easier to find a black stone in the dark, than an honest Israelite by the light of day. The greater part of them gain a livelihood by dealing in second-hand goods, articles of apparel, &c.

The severity of the English laws is every wher« An English shilling is usually reckoned at twenty two cents *oi ourjmoney.j* known. While in their courts innocent persons have been sentenced and executed on inconclusive or circumstantial evidence, the commission of comparatively light offences, brings the culprit to the gallows. The highest punishment next to hanging, is transportation to Botany Bay. In conversation with a clergyman on this point, the author inquired the probable cause of the existence of a law that seemed so contrary to human justice and the Divine institution, and punished so small offences with death. He was informed, that probably more offenders would be sent to New South Wales, were it not for the expense incurred by the government for each transportation. That the severity and frequency of capital punishment has no reforming influence upon the community at large, may be argued from the fact, that at every session of the court, numbers are condemned and cast for execution; from five to seventeen have been turned off at one time.

The punishment for suicide exhibits a striking relic of the barbarism of former ages. It consists in removing the self-murdered man to the centre where four roads cross each other, and digging a large and deep hole, they fix a sharpened stake in the bottom, and pass it through the corpse which is then buried. This savage law is generally evaded by the verdict of the Jury; if they allege insanity to have been the cause of the suicide, Christian burial is authorised. The writer recollects to have read of only one case during his residence in London, where the body was brought naked to the spot, on a board, and deposited in the earth; the disgraceful ceremony of the stake was very properly omitted. The man was a foreigner.

Foggy weather is very common in London. In the winter of 1817-18 they had a day so dark that no business could be done in the houses without candles, and in the streets it was necessary to carry lighted torches before horses and carriages.

As very few people who reside in our country towns can form an adequate idea of the effect produced by the continual passing of the numerous crowds, who attending to business, curiosity, or pleasure, move rapidly along the streets; so the various objects presented to view from day to day are as curious to behold as difficult to describe. The carriages of the great, with one, two, or three footmen hanging on behind, arrayed in splendid liveries; hackney-coaches, stages and carts, coal-waggons and drays, are frequently collected together in such numbers as to become mutual impediments to each other's progress. The lady of quality, with her tall man-servant marching at a respectful distance behind; the coarse, dirty damsel from Billingsgate fish-market, with her basket/of mackerel, salmon, or herring, balanced on her head, resolutely braving the eyes of men, women andjjchildren, while in loudest strains she utters forth the commodity she wishes to sell: the merchant hurrying to his counting house, with stock, per centage, loss and gain revolving in his aching head; the Jew ragpedlar, with bag on shoulder, having little to risk or lose, not even a good name, calls loudly for old clothes to buy; lawyers and doctors; bishops and curates; some in gilded chariots and some on humbler feet, incessantly threaten decay and destruction to the solid pavement. The sober traveller, and the poor captive just let loose in chains from the last ale-house, meet and negociate the terms of passing each other; honest men and knaves, sometimes few and far between, and sometimes near

enough together for the dexterous pick-pocket to lighten his neighbor of watch, pocket book, or silk-handkerchief unperceived —yea, all the varieties of human life, here meet the astonished eye.

Whether it be that the city air in the midst of a dense population is most favorable to health, or not, the females in London are generally accustomed to take exercise in walking that would be considered by the fair daughters of our hills and vales too much for human nature to endure; three, five or ten miles are frequently traveled on foot in visiting, shopping, or gratifying their curiosity. It is a common thing in the beautiful mornings of spring and summer, to Bee troops of fair-haired damsels, their cheeks flushed by the brightest glow of health, come in to market with baskets of fruit on their heads from the distance of eight or ten miles, which having sold, they set out on their return, hardly allowing themselves time to rest or refresh.

CHAPTER V.
Visit to Dublin.—General Remarks on the state of the Irish poor. Carriages. —Castle of Carrickfergus.—Voyage in the Helena.— City of Edinburgh.—Return to London.—Study of Algebra commenced.—Visit of the Allied Sovereigns to the British capital. —Mr. Colburn goes to Paris,

From the time that Mr. Colburn first left home, he had frequently written to his wife describing his situation and prospects. To those who may well wonder that he could at all reconcile himself i o the thought of being absent from his family, consisting of five boys and two girls, who continually needed a father's presence and counsel and authority, it may be proper to say that his absence always filled him with regret. He loved his family, and was of an unusually domestic turn and disposition. The letters which he frequently wrote home from England, uniformly contain such expressions of kind concern and affection as were suitable for an affectionate husband and father: he thought of home, and longed for the approach of a period which he was persuaded would come, when he might return. Is it asked why

then he tarried so long in a foreign land be our plain answer this: he was perfectly confident that the hour drew near when he should return in a manner that'would be honorable to himself, and make every amends to his deserted family for years of separation. The event painfully showed that he was mistaken in his anticipations, but however misguided he might have been, there never was a period at which he could have felt justified in his own mind to abandon his undertaking, and without educating his son come back to his farm.

It appears from letters of his, bearingate August, 1812, that there was some prospect then of a plan being formed, which would meet his wishes and enable him to return to America, leaving his son in London in study. From want of funds, the gentlemen who were engaged in this project had hitherto been unable to bring it into operation. The sale of the portrait did not effect this; the contemplated memoir was suggested, in order to accomplish it. Titled, rich, and scientific personages patronized it, and it was principally at the instance of Professor John Leslie, of Edinburgh, that Mr. Colburn proceeded to Ireland and Scotland. Could the memoir have been published under the proposed patronage of fifteen hundred subscribers, it is most likely that Zerah would have been put to study, while his father returned to Cabot to superintend his interests there. This however was not to be.

It was about the first of September, 1813, that Mr. Colburn and Zerah went from Liverpool to Dublin. The very favorable reception they had met with in London was extended to them by the hospitable inhabitants of this ancient city. During their residence here, they were visited by the first people of the place, and were often invited to partake of the hospitalities of their homes. They received only thirty-two names as subscribers for the book; the principal reason that a larger list was not obtained here, as well as in London, was, that while the gentlemen denominated a Committee permitted their names to be printed on the prospectus in that capacity, probably very limited efforts were made by them to induce people to subscribe: they had their owa interests to pursue. Had they appointed a suitable person to wait on gentlemen at their houses, exhibit the proposals, and request signatures, there is little doubt but what the requisite number might have been obtained. The price of the book would necessarily place it out of the reach of many who would have been. glad to read it; but the first movers of the plan calculated more largely than circumstances would warrant. They designed to have a quarto volume, with a portrait; printed on the best paper, in a style of superior elegance. How many pages they calculated upon is not known, but it must have required a mighty mind to extract matter sufficient to be worth eight dollars, from the history of three years of a child's life, even if that child were Zerah Colburn. The committee nominated in Dublin were Dr. Magee, Dr. Mooney, Dr. Davenport, and Dr. Brinkley, all of them scientific men, and associated in the college.

After they had spent four or five weeks in this city, they went on to Belfast. "There were exhibiting in Dublin, at this same period, a person of such gigantic stature that Mr. Colburn, who' measured six feet, could stand erect under his arm horizontally extended: Miss Honeywell, an American, who was there cutting out watch-papers and other curiosities by the use of her toes. Also, an English woman named Harvey, remarkable for a fair skin, red eyes, and hair glistening like polished metal, nearly white: she had a brother possessing similar peculiarities.

The Irish character has often been described and as often admired; but it is difficult for those who have always been comfortably fed, and clothed, and housed, amid the blessings of civilization, to form an adequate idea of the manner in which these poor, oppressed, and yet light-hearted sons of Erin, live on what many would consider hardly sufficient for their swine, in dwellings (except the heat of a peat fire) less comfortable than we provide for our horses and cattle: here, bearing the human form, and possessing within the germ of every feeling which among the more enlightened, is raised, expanded, and led into the path of noble enterprise and high renown, crushed by oppression and bound in darkness, far from the arts of life, the lights of science, and the brilliant lustre which religion pours upon the world, the poor degraded Irishman lives, contented, and happy, perhaps, that he knows no more. Strange that in so beautiful a clime, on an island so near the very centre of Christendom, so much ignorance, wretchedness and superstition, should exist; but it is to be hoped, and let the Christian pray, that the time may not be far remote, when the Providence of God will raise up a Deliverer, when the blessings of freedom and the joys of salvation will flow in copious streams upon that country.

The degradation alluded to, under which Ireland groans, could, even twenty years ago, show as its legitimate offspring the vice and crime that prevailed. Going with a few friends about seven miles from the city to dine, and returning in the evening, the writer learnt that all in the carriage, except the ladies, were armed with pistols, thinking it very possible that their party might be attacked by highwaymen.

At that period there was one carriage peculiar to Ireland, as the sulky is to our country, called a "jaunting-car." The hind-wheels about three feet in diameter on an axletree no longer: the seats, two in number, were hung on the length of the body, in such a manner that the occupants must sit sideways to the horse, and with their backs toward each other, their feet being within six or eight inches of the ground. To compensate, it would seem, for this unsociable conveyance, they have another vehicle, mounted on two wheels, in shape something like one half of a hogshead cut in two, with a seat running round on the inside; this they aptly call a "sociable."

As in Dublin, so in Belfast, the inhabitants received them kindly. While in Belfast they were invited to visit Carrickfergus, a neighboring village, distant eight Irish miles. This is a small town on the sea-shore. It derives its name from an ancient king Fergus; *carrick* in the Irish language signifying a rock. The principal curiosity here is a castle built at a period of antiquity so remote that no traces of its date can be obtained, though the general opinion is, that it must have stood more than two thousand years. Among the proofs we have that the ancients had arts which have been lost to us in the lapse of centuries, the writer was informed by the resident clergyman that on some occjision, wishing to remove a piece of the massive walls, in order to make some internal alterations, the workmen engaged came in contact with a cement so hard that the best instruments they had were insufficient to penetrate it: all that one could remove in a day being a few broken fragments carried off in his apron. They also show to strangers as another curiosity, a large stone, at the water's edge, on which William, Prince of Orange, first set his foot when landing to deliver Ireland from the oppression of James tho Second.

After tarrying here some days, Mr. Colburn began to make preparations for a passage to Scotland. There was at this time an English sloop of war, the Helena, commanded by Captain Henry Montresor, cruising up and down the channel in quest of American vessels. Captain Montresor, learning Mr. C.'s desire, immediately offered to carry him over. As he was not quite ready to go, the Captain went off on another cruise, and returning again in two days, took the Americans on board, and treated them in the most friendly and gentlemanly manner.— Among the numerous questions the officers proposed to Zerah, he was requested to give the square of 53,053; to which he correctly answered, 2,814,620,809. When landed at Greenock, the Helena lay at anchor, till about sunset, and learning that a Privateer called "The true blooded Yankee" had been seen, immediately gave chase, but did not overtake her. The "writer takes pleasure in mentioning circumstances of this kind, in support of the high opinion he entertains of the English character.

Being landed at Greenock, almost the first object that met the author's eye, while going to the house of entertainment, was an officer of the Highlanders, having the soldier's cap, coat and sword, with the plaid shirt reaching to the knees, which were bare, and stockings below;—rather a cool costume for November. They immediately took the stage for Glasgow, but made no tarry in that city, Edinburgh, the capital of the North, being the place of their present destination.

Edinburgh consists of two parts, called the Old and the New Town, connected by a bridge thrown across a dry and broad valley. It is in the Old Town, that the houses of thirteen stories are found. We believe, however, that the true state of the case is this: such houses are built on a side hill so steep, that while the upper side may not contain more than seven or eight stories, the lower side in a few instances numbers thirteen. There are many with ten stories; still more with eight and six. They build without exception of hewn stone. The writer doea not recollect to have seen in Edinburgh, Glasgow, or Greenock, one house constructed of any other material. The Old Town contains the College edifice, erected within twenty-five years, Holyrood Palace, and a number of other buildings, venerable for age.

The Castle stands at the upper end of High street, powerful by its size and strength, and inaccessible »n the other sides by reason of steep rocks, on whose elevated summits it lifts its majestic pride. The streets are often narrow, laid out with little or no attention to neatness.. Indeed the inference would be forcible upon every mind, that they were anxious to collect the greatest number of souls on the smallest possible quantity of land. Except the wealthy and independent, the families of Edinburgh and Glasgow generally occupy but one story each. To the inquiry why the inhabitants build their houses so lofty, it has been replied, that in feudal times of frequent turmoil, war, and bloodshed, exposed to frequent inroads of the neighboring chieftains, they were de-

sirous of contracting the limits of their town, so as to be near the Castle, their common defence.

The New Town of Edinburgh is generally admitted to be the finest city in Europe. As it regards regularity, uniformity, and a noble style in the houses, commodious width of streets, and grandeur of public buildings, it approaches nearest to a perfect pattern of all the writer has ever seen. Its situation is romantic, among towering hills, which are not so near as to bury the prospect afforded from the city.

The Scottish character is that of an industrious and persevering, hospitable and friendly people more easily given to superstitious notions of the mar« vellous than the English. Their winters are morn severe than in England; when the writer was re» turning by land to London in the unusually cokiS winter of 1813-14, a passage was obtained for the stage in many places only by shovelling out the roads, and piling up the snow on each side as high as the stage. Their carriages all move on wheels, the use of any thing like a sleigh being utterly unknown among them.

Among the distinguished persons who noticed the youthful calculator, were Dugald Stewart, Professor Playfair, Dr. Brewster, and Dr. Macknight. Some. addition was here made to the subscription list, but the same impediments which had formerly hindered, still prevented its extensive enlargement. After remaining in Edinburgh long enough to gratify the curiosity of the people, he went to Glasgow, where he tarried a few weeks, and concluding that no very efficient patronage might be expected, his father made arrangements for leaving the North to return to London, where they arrived in the early part of March, 1814.

Having by this time visited the principal cities the British islands, furnishing the inhabitants witf an opportunity of personal examination of the things whereof they had heard so much, and also of contributing such patronage as they were disposed to offer, Mr. Colburn and his son called on Mr. Montagu on their arrival in London, to give an

account of their journeyings and success, and to ask counsel as to their future course. As usual the lawyer received them with kindness, and expressed the greater satisfaction at seeing them, because he had heard that Zerah died on the journey. Matters were not in the situation that they could have desired. The number of subscribers for the book, which after all the efforts made by Mr. C. amounted only to four hundred, did not appear sufficient to warrant their proceeding with the publication. The agency of the Committee, who had volunteered their services, had been merely nominal so far, as all the names received had been collected by Mr. C. While he was absent from London, not one in addition had been obtained by either of the four gentlemen associated. There seemed to be no great prospect of further enlargement in London: and the prospect was equally small of profitably continuing an exhibition of the boy. What course was now most eligible did not distinctly appear, but as Mr. Montagu still held out a flattering prospect, it was deemed best to be guided by his judgment. Hitherto the plans devised for patronage had seemed to say, like the Boston Indenture, "Do you raise the funds necessary, and then we will educate your son." His education, except in reading and writing, had hitherto been neglected, on account of his being exhibited, but it was now recommended that he should commence a course of mathematical studies. In pursuance of this advice, aprivate instructer was engaged, and Hutton's Algebra commenced.

This may be a suitable place for introducing a few remarks concerning the mind of Zerah in regard to other things than mental calculation. As might be expected from the nature of his early gift, he ever had a taste for figures. To answer questions by the mere operation of mind, though perfectly easy, was not anything in which he ever took satisfaction; for, unless when questioned, his attention was not engrossed by it at all. The study of Arithmetic was not particularly easy to him, but it afforded a very pleasing employment, and even now, were he in a situation to feel justified in such a course, he should be gratified to spend his time in pursuits of this nature. The faculty which he possessed, as it increased and strengthened by practice, so by giving up exhibition, began speedily to depreciate. This was not as some have supposed, on account of being engaged in study; it is more probable to him that the study of any branch that included the use and practice of figures would have served to keep up the facility and readiness of his mind. The study of Algebra, while he attended to it, was very pleasant, but when just entering upon the more abstruse rules of the first part, he was taken away from his books and carried to France.

The attention of the European nations was now particularly directed to that country. After a long and sanguinary struggle, they had succeeded in dethroning the French Emperor, and peace was established. As a natural consequence, the intercourse between the citizens of England and France, so long interrupted, was resumed, and such as had commercial interests to secure, or were fond of traveling, speedily embraced the opportunity of visiting Paris. From some cause the idea was suggested to Mr. Montagu, that there was one place where Mr. Colburn had not been, and he advised him immediately to go to Paris. The counsel doubtless proceeded from friendly motives, but in the present state of things was exceedingly improper. After having been carried round three years and a half for the purposes of exhibition, he was just commencing his studies, being nearly ten years old; his father and he were perfectly unacquainted with the country, the language and manners of the French; their pecuniary resources were scanty; every thing seemed to be entirely against such a measure. Whether these considerations presented themselves to Mr. Montagu or not, he strongly urged Mr. Colburn to go, and offered letters of introduction. Having been long accustomed to listen too much to the advice of others, whom he considered to have more knowledge and experience than himself, Mr. Colburn reluctantly consented, yet made no calculation on staying long in the French capital.

The spring of 1814 was a period of general Jubilee in London. The people, especially such a part of them as considered Napoleon to be an usurper and a tyrant, while they rejoiced in his downfall, were flattered by the great success of the British arms. The Duke of Wellington, whose conduct for a few years past has not entitled him to much praise as an able and popular statesman, had thus far been known only in his military character, and stood high in the public estimation. The exiled Prince of Bourbon, afterwards known by the name of Louis the eighteenth, had come from his sequestered residence in England, to behold the kings who had combined to restore him to the throne of his fathers, and greet them in their triumph. The Emperor Alexander of Russia, the King of Prussia, General Blucher, Platoff, and others of noble name and high reputation, both in the field and the cabinet, passed over from Paris to the English court, to partake of the hospitality of the Prince Regent, and share in the festivities that were held. Probably there never was a time before when so many kings and potentates met on British soil, if indeed on any other. During their visit, it was one continued gala. Triumphal arches were erected, frequent entertainments were given, royal reviews of the troops were attended; every thing in fact was done which a princely generosity could invent to honor the occasion, and to furnish the guests on their departure, with exalted views of the English nation; two of the Cossacks who marched under the Hetman Platoff to the walls of Paris, accompanied the train to England, and were to many, objects of curiosity as great as the American boy had ever excited; they were men of a large frame, rough features, dressed in coarse blue woollen, wearing a long beard, and carrying a pike or lance about twelve feet in length, which they exhibited great dexterity in handling.

Among the numerous amusements of that day, one thing however was done, which appeared to show that John Bull, so long accustomed to conquest, was anxious if he could not obtain it, at least to revel in the dreams of victory. A large stream of water in Hyde Park, was selected as the scene of the great exploit. A number of boats, about the size of small fishing vessels, were built and rigged like ships of war; one division was termed the British fleet, the other the American armament. After several weeks of preparation, during which the public Journals frequently published the occasional dispatches received from this fresh-water flotilla, thus furnishing a frequent source of laughter to the public; after much of naval manœuvering in miniature, the day appointed for the grand, eventful fight, came on. Thousands, both great and small, assembled to witness the sight, which, had it originated in the minds of little boys-at school, might have elicited a smile of approbation from their seniors, but sanctioned as it was by the first men of the first nation of Europe, was too simple and foolish a boast. The baby squadrons met, and after burning a great quantity of powder—(the.y had no shot,) to increase the national debt and burthen, the ridiculous scene was closed by the London Yankees striking their flags, as they were *iuaf* ucted to do at a certain period of the performance. Then Johnny felt nicely, and after many praises to the skill and valor of his sailors, went home well pleased, thinking perhaps that now the decisive blow was struck, and that America would no longer boast of independent, sovereign rights, and power. One little item it seems they in their martial ardor had wisely overlooked; they forgot to put trueborn Americans in the boats allotted to our Navy.. At any time such an exhibition would have appeared empty and vain to a judicious eye; but at this period of the American war, when as yet the English had gained no important advantage on our seas, and finally were compelled to renounce their vain pretensions and conclude a peace so honorable to our country, it was calculated to represent their wisdom and greatness of soul in a very disparaging light.

As well as a peculiarity of mind, Zerah Colbura had a slight one of the body, being furnished with five fingers on each hand and six toes on each foot. Whether this be a proof of direct lineal descent from Philistine blood or not (see 1 Chronicles xx. 6.), it is a mark which for a number of generations has been in the family. His father and two of his sons were equipped all round with the extra complement. After their return from Scotland the fingers were taken off by Dr. Carlisle. He was very anxious to remove the toes likewise, on account of their probable inconvenience to him when learning to dance; but as yet there has been no trouble on that account.

CHAPTER VI.

Mr. Colburn arrives in Paris.—Situation of things in that capital.— Visit to the Institute.—Dr. Gall.—Washington Irving.—Zerah is placed at the Lyceum Napoleon.—Removed from thence to London, in February, 1816.

Leaving London in the month of July, 1814, Mr. Colburn proceeded by stage to Dover. In their company happened to be their Edinburgh friend, Professor Leslie, who spent a good part of the time between morning and the hour of sailing, in measuring the altitude of the white cliffs along the shore. It is said that in a clear day, they can distinctly see from the British to the French coasts, a distance of twenty one miles. However this may be, they were between three and four hours in crossing the channel in a packet sloop named (probably in allusion to the recent peace) "The perfect Union."

Being landed in Calais, they started for the capital of the "Great Nation." The carriage in which they engaged places was one very different from all that they had formerly been accustomed to see. It was furnished with a long body, three seats on the inside, and a covered seat at the fore end. This however was not appropriated to the driver; no: he, a sprightly youngster, wearing a coarse frock, hair long enough behind to be fastened up in a queue containing three or four pounds of lead to make it lie down on the neck, and a monstrous pair of wooden boots, or at least strengthened with wood, and leather, and iron, into which he thrust his foot and shoe, mounted one of the wheel horses and taking the reins into his hands, drove three leaders abreast at a rapid rate along. It was very fashionable to wear the hair loaded with lead, especially among the lower orders. Perhaps they wanted something to keep their volatile heads any where within bounds. It was a common story in 1814, that many of the soldiers being out of balk, took the lead from their necks, to cast into bullets, at the siege of Paris.

Being arrived in that city, Mr. Colburn found a number of American gentlemen, some of them occasional residents, and some permanently established in various departments of commerce. William H. Crawford was then our Minister at the Court of France; George Washington Irving, since renowned as an author, having finished his mission to Spain, was in that capital. They very generally subscribed to the book, and for the most part, paid their subscription down. Indeed such assistance was very soon necessary, as Mr. Colburn had but little money on reaching Paris; and besides, the French people manifested very little interest in the calculations performed by his son.

The Prospectus which had been used in London, was translated into French, and some efforts made to give it a circulation, but to little purpose. Whether it were principally owing to the native frivolity and lightness of the French people, or to the painful effect produced by the defeat of t heir armies and the restoration of the exiled Louis XVIII. cannot be correctly tated; probably it was owing to the former. Still, their recent subjugation by combined Europe, and the forcible imposition of a king upon them, who possessed not one striking claim to their veneration, by a Power which had long been the object of their jealousy, bore heavily upon the minds of many. No national prejudice could be cited as the reason of their neglecting the calculating boy, for friendship was the predominant feeling they cherished towards our country. While they remembered with sorrow their recent defeat, they beheld with indignation the throngs of English travellers, now after a long interval visiting their country, and displaying, at least to their eyes, the pride of victory, and supercilious contempt of the vanquished.

According to the principles recognized among hereditary sovereigns, the new monarch—in some engravings styled "The Desired," and in others caricatured to excess—commenced his reign by an attempt to efface from French recollection, their former ruler and his splendid achievements. Many of the streets, named from some circumstance connected with Napoleon's days of triumph and honor, received names more congenial with Bourbon feelings. The schools under the patronage of the government changed their titles. The statue of Napoleon was removed from the pillar of the Place Vendftme, and the white flag substituted in its place. Instead of the hoary veterans, who made the Imperial Guard a formidable phalanx, the king organized for his body guard a company of young men, more accustomed to the recreations of peace, than the tumult and toil of the tented field.

The palace of the Thuileries, long accustomed to the simplicity of the warrior's table and household, was now furnished with all the officers of luxury, fashion, indolence, and extravagance. The Catholic religion was supported by all the influence and patronage of the new establishment, and a course of policy adopted, directly tending to disgust a nation, which notwithstanding the inordinate ambition of the Corsican adventurer, still remembered with delight-the reformation he had introduced in many abuses, the numerous works he accomplished for the benefit of Paris, and his warlike exploits for securing the glory of the "Great Nation." The effeminacy, gluttony, and intemperance of the old king, were with many a theme of vituperation. They called him the "Fat hog," while he, retired within the pomp of *his* palace, and surrounded by cooks and friars, heeded them not. Poor man! such a state of things existed, that it need excite little surprise, that escaping from Elba, the Emperor should pass through France without interruption, and find the Parisians ready to receive him with open arms.

Immediately after Mr. Colburn arrived in Paris, at the instigation of some American friends, he engaged a dwelling, consisting of eleven rooms, some of them very large, at the rent of 2000 francs per annum, and purchased furniture to the amount of 1600 more. What his advisers could have contemplated in such a course, remains unknown; Mr. C. had little money, and little prospect of getting any. It should be mentioned in vindication of his friends, that they paid up the rent, while he occupied the rooms, and afterwards when he removed from Paris, the furniture was taken back by the upholsterer.

A French teacher was engaged to instruct Zerah in the French language. Being only ten years old, and having every facility afforded him, it would have been strange if he did not make good proficiency: the teacher was dismissed after three or four months, when his pupil was able to converse with considerable ease.

By the influence of William Temple Franklin, (grandson to the Doctor, it is believed,) an introduction was obtained for the boy before the members of the French " Institute," by whom he was examined. Three months had now elapsed that he had not been exhibited, but had given his attention to study; even in this short space, it was observable that he had lost in the quickness of his computations. When examined at this time, he was much longer in attaining to the answer of questions than ever before. On retiring, they favored him with a copy of their Journal of that day in reference to him, bearing date August 4, 1814, and signed by their secretary, Delanobre. The celebrated mathematician, La Place, was present at that time.

Dr. Gall, well known as the author of the system of Craniology, was then in Paris, and by means of hia tutor, Zerah was introduced to him, without the Doctor's having any previous intimation of the character of his visiter. Being requested by Mr. C. he proceeded to examine the cranium of his subject, and readily discovered on the sides of the

eyebrows certain protuberances and peculiarities which indicated the presence of a faculty for computation. The early gift of the boy was then described, and the Doctor was desirous of taking a cast in plaster from his face.

Early in the month of February, Mr. Colburn was requested by letter to take his son to the house of Count Guizot, secretary to the Minister of Internal Affairs, who at an early period of Zerah's history, had introduced a brief notice of him in a book he had published. We insert his letter. as a specimen of the complimentary style of the French.

"To Mr. Colburn, father. "Sir,

"Persuaded that I have only done justice to the qualities (endowments) of your son, by naming him with approbation in "The Annals of Education," published by me, I can but be charmed, to receive you and him at my house on the evening of Wednesday."

Then after all his titles written out in full, his name was signed, "Guizot."

English flattery is sometimes fulsome; but the French use the superlative degree much more freely.

A Jew broker called on Mr. C. and after some conversation, invited his son to call at his house some evening, and take tea; it so happened that he went on Saturday. Mr. B. was very friendly and courteous, but after the evening was nearly spent, perceiving no preparation that indicated the approach of eating, the boy took his leave, uncertain what it might mean. He afterwards learnt that the seeming neglect with which he had been treated, was owing to a Jewish scruple, which forbids their eating with Christians during any part of their Sabbath.

It seemed to be an opinion with some of his American friends, that Zerah might enjoy greater advantages for obtaining an education in Paris than in any other place where he had been, though no organized, connected plan, was struck out to accomplish this. As he had made good proficiency in the French language, the study of the German was commenced, but it did not strike his mind favorably, and he made little progress in it. After things had stood

in this situation for a few months, and perceiving no prospect of any regular plan of patronage, Mr. Colburn left his son in Paris, and went to London, to see what advice or aid he might receive from his friends associated in the Book Committee. The matter had slumbered with them: nothing had been done. Being incited by the presence of Mr. C. to make some new movement, they inserted the following item in the Prospectus: "The education of the boy, since the first publication of this Prospectus, has been carefully attended to, (by whom or at whose expense 1) and his progress in mathematics and in languages is truly astonishing;" (rather stronger expressions than the fact would warrant; and then) "but it has become necessary that some portion of the subscription should be paid to Mr. Colburn, to enable him to continue his son's education." "The subscribers are therefore requested to pay the amount of their subscriptions to Mr. Thomas Biggs, who is duly authorized under the hands of Sir James Mackintosh, M. P., Mr. Basil Montagu, K. Finley, Esq. M. P. and Sir Humphrey Davy, to receive the same." This man, Thomas Biggs, accordingly called upon a large number of the subscribers; on the credit of the subscription Mr. Colburn borrowed one hundred pounds of Kirkman Finley, and returned to Paris, encouraged in regard to the arrangement.

As already stated, Washington Irving was at that time in Paris; soon after his return from London, Mr. C. called upon him, and made known his situation. Thus becoming acquainted with the subject of this memoir, Mr. Irving was led to take a decided interest in promoting his father's wishes; the education of the boy. Soon after Mr. I. took the boy to the house of Mrs. Fenwick, a lady well known in the circle of. American society in Paris, where were assembled several gentlemen of the army. General Haxo was one. The names of the others are not remembered. The General seemed quite pleased with his answering questions, and gave him the usual French salute, a kiss.

The first intimation after this introduction which the father had of the success of Mr. Irving's exertions, v/as a letter from that gentleman, stating, that the matter which had been brought before these officers, had by them been presented to the Minister of the Interior, and receiving his sanction, was to go in the form of a regularly certified memorial before the King, requesting his assent in establishing the youth at one of the Government schools, formerly denominated the Lyceum Napoleon, but now the Royal College of Henry the Fourth: but before the King's consent was obtained, Napoleon returned from Elba, and the matter in its present form was ended. However, they persevered in their efforts; the Emperor was applied to in his behalf, and the necessary approbation obtained. Accordingly he entered that seminary May 30th, 1815. He was informed that the Emperor had signified a desire to see him, but the sudden reverse produced in his fortunes by the defeat at Waterloo, prevented this.

In order that the bounty of the French government may be duly appreciated, it is proper here to observe that the school in question was designed for the general education of the scholar, a knowledge of reading being the only requisite for admission. And even this seemed to be set aside in the case of one student, nearly eighteen years old, who was there, trying almost in vain to learn reading and writing. Masters were employed to teach writing, French grammar, a critical acquaintance with their language, Latin, Greek, Mathematics, &c. &c. After this course of study had been honorably passed through, the laborious student might be a candidate for admission into the Polytechnic school, where he might pursue studies more decidedly of a warlike character.

The annual expense of the school, comprising every thing—board, clothing, books, tuition, medical treatment if needed, &c. &c. was 1000 livres (200 dollars). The purchase of an outfit with which to enter, clad and furnished in every necessary, amounted to 750 livres (150 dollars). But this latter sum, the officers of the establishment expected Mr. C. to pay. When this should be paid, his son might remain in the institution until his studies were completed.

The seminary in which Zerah was now placed was in almost every respect a specimen of his genius, who at the military college in Brienne laid the foundation of his greatness, and commenced his career, afterwards so remarkable and important to the interests of Europe. The scholars were habited in a blue uniform, with the Eagle of France on the buttons, a large cocked hat, and tri-colored cockade. They rose and slept, studied and played, ate and refrained from eating, at beat of drum. In winter they rose before day to commence their studies. They were detained in their school room not only when met in class for recitation, but also during certain hours allotted to preparing their lessons, under the care of a teacher. Three times a day they were let out to play.

Their breakfast consisted of dry bread and water. Dinner at noon consisted of soup, not made in the beet culinary style, meat, and something else as a third course to finish the meal. At dinner and supper, their drink consisted of their country-wine mixed with water; this they called "Abundance." They had a luncheon of dry bread at four, and supper at eight, when they went to bed. Previous to undressing at night, and before leaving the dormitory in the morning, one of the boys was called upon to repeat the Lord's prayer. No correction with a stick, or any other weapon, was allowed; but sometimes a tutor was unmercifully liberal with his hand. Imprisonment for days, in case of a flagrant offence; dry bread at dinner or at supper; withholding from the scholars permission to go home once in a fortnight, and spending the hours allotted to recreation in writing off one, two, or more, hundred lines from some Latin author, were among the punishments most in use. Expulsion was seldom resorted to.

Their hours of recreation were spent under the immediate superintendance of an officer of the establishment: no quarreling, boxing, or fighting, wag allowed. They had two Sabbaths in the week, Thursday and Sunday, on which study was suspended—at least the recitations in class—and the Romish Mass attended in the college chapel by all except six or seven, who claimed exemption on account of being Protestants: after which, in pleasant weather, they were led out to walk in various parts of the city, or the adjacent suburbs. On all other occasions, they were confined by bars and bolts from any intercourse with the populous city, and all its temptations.

With a view to render the scholars hardy and robust, any thing like a surtout or great coat was not furnished by the stewards, and the use of them in the winter discountenanced. To such as preferred the improvement of their own minds to the relaxations and amusements so frequently prized by youth, Some time after the king's return in 1815, a son of General Savary was expelled for disloyalty in-writing on the wall, "Long Kvs tin Emperor." this seminary afforded peculiar advantages. It is in the author's mind a question, if there be in England or America any school that can compare with the French Lyceum. Study was made an active business; a discipline (not nominal merely,) was enforced; retirement was inevitable; board, clothing, and every other necessary were at hand—all within the limit of two hundred dollars per annum.

After the battle which terminated the hopes of Napoleon in 1815, while the Parisians were expecting the approach of the allied armies, the scholars received permission to go out to a certain spot on one of the roads that led to the city, and dig trenches to 'fortify the passage into their capital. With one consent, and frequent shouts of "Vive l'Empereur!" they sallied forth, the young man and the child seven or eight years old, and spent the day in that employment. With little exception, the youthful community were warm in their attachment to the Imperial government.

The prospect was now more flattering than it had ever been before for Zerah Colburn to receive such an education as would qualify him, if education could do it, to be useful in the scientific world.

While in the Lyceum, he attended to the study of L'Homond's French Grammar, writing and Latin; but as no provision had been made to pay the expenses of his outfit, his situation was not so permanent as might have been wished. Mr. Colburn being now at ease, and at liberty, in relation to his son, returned to London to attend to the subscription business.

It was late in the summer when he arrived in England. He found that Thomas Biggs, the authorized agent, had actually collected about one third of the subscriptions: when called upon to account for receipts, it appeared that he had appropriated to his own use the whole sum; he was a poor man, so that a legal course would have recovered nothing, and Mr. Montagu manifested no inclination to point out a course by which the loss might be retrieved. Mr. Colburn began to discover that the committee men were relaxing in their tone of interest, as if they had long enough been concerned in the business, and being now indisposed to support him in a loss which they had indirectly brought upon him, the whole undertaking, as far as they were concerned, fell to the ground.

Wounded, discouraged, and wholly ignorant what course to pursue, Mr. C. applied to some persons who had not previously taken a very active part in patronizing him. He disclosed to them the delinquency of Biggs, as well as the establishment of his son at the Lyceum. They manifested much sympathy for his trials, but instead of rejoicing that he had found such friends in Paris, they appeared to be mortified that after all the high professions and anticipations of patronage in London, they had done nothing, and the subject of their talk had been taken by the hand

"It never should be said that his friends in London bad not. succeeded in efficiently patronizing him." But what could be done *l* Old plans had become ineffectual; some new one must be started. At length the idea suggested itself to them of raising two hundred pounds annually for six years, to defray the expenses of his education. They prepared their prospectus under the names of Ge-

orge Bridges, Esq, Alderman, Sir James Shaw, and one or two others as a committee, to manage the business, and a few names were obtained on this plan.

The idea of removing his son from the Lyceum was not agreeable to Mr. Colburn, but the persuasion of his new friends, added to his inability to procure the sum due for his outfit, (750 francs) at last induced him to assent to their proposition.

Having formerly become acquainted with an American named Goldthwaite, at that time in London, and wishing to go to Paris, Mr. C. called on him to

One of them remarked, see if he would call at the Lyceum, take his son away, and bring him back to London. He agreed to do it if he were furnished with the means requisite. Mr. C. accordingly borrowed twelve pounds to pay the traveling expenses of his son, and he departed.

Goldthwaite was in truth a poor miserable wretch. He went on to Paris, called at the school, and stated his business to Zerah. He made known in part his father's wishes, and gave it as his opinion that it would be much better for him to tarry where he was, and pursue his studies. He also requested him to direct a letter to his father stating that he chose to remain in Paris, which letter he would see safely forwarded. The fact was, the rogue had applied Mr. Colburn's money to his own use, and took this course to furnish himself with a plausible excuse for returning without Zerah, as if he had refused to leave the school. Zerah suspected nothing of all this, and wrote to his father stating that he should like to revisit London, though if it were for the best, he was willing to remain where he was. Goldthwaite returned to England, delivered his JpJtter, a»d Mr. Colburn immediately set off himself, took his son out of school, and arrived in London in February, 1816, CHAPTER VII.

Manners of the French people.—New Year's day.—The Morgue.— Dautun. —Wild boy.—Fountains.—Gallery of the Louvre.—Return of Napoleon.— Ney.—Labedoyere.—Lavalette.

The period which it was the

writer'sfortune to spend in France, was a very interesting one. As already intimated, there were numbers in that country who could not reconcile themselves to the great changes produced among them by the hated intervention of foreign power. Still the majority of the people seemed disposed to make the best of their troubles, if indeed they considered them to be roubles, while the necessary business of life proceeded as before; so did gaiety, recreation, and folly. Indeed this would seem to be the very atmosphere in which a Frenchman lives and breathes and moves. Residing in an elegant city, whose aspect seems peculiarly adapted to the lighter pursuits of life; situated in a delightful climate, and furnished with all the variety of objects that can exhilarate, or induce forgetfulness of what is unpleasant and painful; in the midst of spacious walks, luxuriant gardens, shows, amusements of every kind, while the various arts of elegant and refined life present their noblest works to charm the eye, and gratify the sense.

As might be expected from these circumstances, taken in connection with the low state of religious feeling or information, it must be confessed that while there are many names who do honor to France, still there are many things in the allowed practice of the Parisians, which set them in a very dubious light, as it regards strictness of morality, and a high regard for the spiritual power and influence of the Gospel. This may not be wondered at, considered as a eommon circumstance among a large proportion of the inhabitants of every country; but to him who remembers the impieties which characterized their Revolution, it may be matter of inquiry whether their present situation at least be not a necessary effect in the order of those heaven-daring causes. Perhaps instead of wondering at their present degradation as to morality and religion, we may rather with gratitude admire the sustaining mercy of the Almighty, whom they so highly provoked, that He did not root them up, as a nation, not scattering, but destroying by one general extermination.

As may be expected from the preceding remarks, the Sabbath is little regarded as a day of religious acts. Let it not be inferred from this that they do not repair to their splendid churches, and bow to their saints and Patrons: all good Catholics do this; but in connection with this, it is for all their citizens a day of unusual festivity. Artisans, mechanics, and all.others whose employments have prevented them-pursuing their pleasure during the week, now come forth in all the buoyancy of unrestrained inclination,' to take once more their fill of such various delights as they covet, or their city affords. The theatres are open; the public promenades are frequented; music and dancing are heard and seen, and an apparent recklessness of things past, and things to come, sensibly prevails. It is no uncommon thing to see in the public gardens parentsleading forth their children, and encouraging them to group together and show their agility in the dance. Gambling houses are open; coffee-houses thronged, and vanity with its atendant evils prevails, without any effort made or intimated by the constituted authorities to regulate or reform.

One of their greatest festivals is the commencement of the New Year; not indeed distinguished by any religious rites, but celebrated with annual rejoicing as Christmas in England, or Thanksgiving days in our country. Parents and children reciprocate vis its; friends meet together; presents are interchanged; superiors and their dependants mutually greet each other. The porter of the house in which the writer lived was a man who had possessed some consequence before the Revolution, but being stripped of all his property in the disasters of that bloody period, he was reduced to the necessity of supporting himself by a servant's life. On the morning of January 1, 1816, while finishing breakfast, Mr. Colburn was called to the door by the ringing of his bell; he started to open it. In walked a man and woman sumptuously arrayed in the fashion of 1780; wonder seized their minds to know who these illustrious guests might be. Their first salutation was to offer the kiss of love to Mr.

Colburn, who retreated from the embrace, as well as a young Irishman who was living with him in the capacity of Interpreter. It was by this time discovered that these who made their morning call, were no less personages than the porter and his wife, arrayed in the garments they wore on the day when they plighted hands and hearts to each other, some forty years before. They had come to offer their congratulations on the return of the New Year.

The greeting of Frenchmen when they meet, is a kiss. It is a prevailing custom to see friends who meet in the street, or elsewhere, fling their arms around each other's necks, and press their bearded lips together.

There are in Paris several hospitals for the reception of the suffering poor. One building, called the Morgue, is, we believe, in its use peculiar to Paris; it is designed for the reception of such dead bodies as are found in any part of the city, which being deposited there by the proper officers, are exposed to be recognized by their friends, who if they have lost a relative in any mysterious manner, go to this place, and take care of their remains. At one time, the writer went to the Morgufe, and saw three corpses, one of which had evidently suffered violence in death.

In the beginning of 1815, a circumstance took place that excited much interest in Paris. A surgeon in the army, named Dautun, was arrested at a gambling house in the Palais Royal, on the testimony of a scar on his wrist. Some time previous, the officers of the night had found while passing on their rounds, in the different parts of the city, four parcels tied up. One contained the head, another the trunk, a third the thighs, and a fourth the legs and arms of a man. In the teeth, tightly compressed, was a piece of human flesh, apparently torn out in the dying struggle. The parts were collected, and put together in their regular order and exhibited for a number of days at the Morgue. The mystery which involved this dark transaction excited quite an interest, Sand numbers went to behold the corpse. The general and only conviction was, that he must

have been murdered; but for a number of weeks no clue was obtained to elicit information on the subject. When it became improper to keep the body longer above ground, a cast in plaster was taken, fully representing the murdered victim, and this remained a much longer time for the public to see. At length Dautun happened to be engaged in gambling at the Palais Royal: he played high and lost; calling for liquor to drink, and angry because the waiter was somewhat tardy, when he came with it, Dautun emptied the glass and threw it at the waiter. It was shivered into a thousand pieces, and a fragment was carried into Dautun's wrist, under the cuff of his coat. The spectators gathered round, and learning the accident, wished to see the gash; he drew down his sleeve, and firmly pressed it round his wrist; they insisted on seeing it, he obstinately refused. By this course, the bystanders were at length led to suppose that something mysterious was involved in his conduct, and they determined at all events to see his wrist. By force they pushed up his sleeve, and behold, a scar, recently healed, as if made by the tearing out of flesh, appeared. The landlord had been at the Morgue, had seen the murdered man with the flesh between his teeth, and it struck him in a moment that that flesh was torn from this man's wrist. Charging them to keep him safe, he hastened to call in the legal authorities, and arrested him.

In the event, Dautun confessed that being quartered at Sedan, and out of money, he came to Paris to try some adventure. Knowing that his brother had a large sum' by him, directly on his arrival, he went to his lodgings in a retired part of the city, about eight in the evening. He entered the house, unnoticed by the porter, and passing to his apartment, found his brother asleep. He immediately commenced his work of death; his brother waking up defended himself, but, in addition to the surprise and horror of the moment, being in a feeble state of health, all the desperation of his struggle was overpowered. In the scuffle, ho tore out the flesh. Being killed the surgeon cut up the body, tied it up in four parcels as before mentioned, secured the money and retired.

He also confessed that eleven months previous he had murdered an aunt, who was living with a second husband, to obtain money. Her husband was arrested and imprisoned for a number of months, but as nothing appeared to criminate him, he had been discharged. The writer saw the unhappy fratricide on his way from prison to the place of execution.

While Zerah was at the Lyceum Napoleon, a Catholic clergyman, with whom he had become acquainted in Dublin, called upon him and took him to visit a neighboring family. One of the household was a young man who had been found in the forests four or five years previous. When first discovered, he was perfectly naked, squatted down in the mire. On the approach of his discoverers he fled on all fours, as a wild animal.» They pursued and succeeded in securing him, almost dead with fear. He was judged to be at that time about fourteen years of age, but was unable to utter any articulate sound; he subsisted upon the spontaneous productions of the forest, roots, nuts, &c. and except his form in no respect differed from the brutish inhabitants of the woods. He was taken to Paris, placed in a private family, and every exertion was made to instruct him. He had not been able to speak, but in writing he had made considerable improvement. Specimens of his penmanship were shown: his habits and manners were gentle and inoffensive; but no traces had ever been discovered of his birth or mysterious exposure, though it was supposed to have been the deed of unnatural parents.

With all the defect of French morality, the author is of the opinion that as a nation they are much less addicted to intoxication than the English. During the eighteen months that he resided in that metropolis, he remembers to have *seen* but ono drunken man in the streets: in London such a sight is very common. This may be partly owing to the quality of their common wines, which are very cheap, and much used,—as freely as porter and cider in other countries. The

public fountains are very numerous, scattered over every part of the city, where there seems to be a space sufficient not otherwise appropriated. The water is collected, and by means of pipes, thrown up to a considerable height in the air, producing a very grateful sensation to the eye, and on the temperature of a summer atmosphere.

Napoleon was a munificent patron of the arts and sciences. While he gave liberal encouragement to men of genius, he seemed anxious to furnish all with an opportunity for improvement. Among his various Efforts, it may be mentioned that the remarkable collection of curious and scientific objects made at tlifferent times, under his direction, in his campaigns abroad, and deposited in Paris, were mostly free, for the inspection of all. The Garden of Plants, with all its treasures of botanical knowledge, was accessible to any. The Menagerie of wild beasts and birds, within the precincts of the Garden, was public. The galleries of Paintings in the Louvre, and also in the Luxembourg Palaces, were thrown open, while rich and poor, the gay Parisian belle or English Nobleman, as well as the sooty chimney-sweeper, with an equal right surveyed the rich specimens of Art before them.

It is not so in London: the Royal Menagerie at the tower is kept from the vulgar eye, and their extensive. cabinet of curiosities in the British Museum, is not to be seen by those who are too poor to dress in a respectable manner. Their cabinet contains munmies and hieroglyphics from Egypt, statues from. V Greece and Rome, articles of apparel and weapons of war from the various savage nations in the Pacific, from Greenland, Kamschatca, &c. and an immense variety of stuffed beasts and birds from everypart of the globe, besides many relics of antiquity found in the British dominions.

The city of Paris differs much in its aspect frop. the British capital. Though in a Frenchman's eye, it be the first among the nations in all respects, still we think that London exceeds it in general con. venience, and cleanliness. Yet the public edifices are more splendid,

some of them ancient, and many are the lasting monuments of Napoleon's efforts to adorn the place of his residence.

The return of the emperor from his honorable banishment at Elba in March, 1815, afforded another opportunity of contemplating the singular volatility of the French character. With many it seemed to be a matter of little moment who filled the throne: the same voices that sounded a welcome loud and long to Louis XVIII. in 1814, were now in excellent tune to shout "Long live Napoleon" on the twentyfirst of March, 1815, the day after he arrived in Paris; and when the royal runaway came back the second time, their accommodating loyalty could still say, "King, live forever."

In company with thousands, on that day the author had an opportunity of beholding the man, whose name so long had filled Europe with terror. "How did he look?" is an inquiry to which he is not prepared to give a direct reply. Of all the likenesses which he has seen during the last nine years, only one conveys a proper representation of his features and expression of countenance. Let it suffice to say that he beheld in Napoleon a face so strongly marked by the hand of Nature in her most elevated and gifted mood, as seemingly to solve the mystery why an obscure islander should by the superiority of his genius, rapidly rise from the lower grades of life, to an eminence envied by his competitors, dreaded by his foes, and gazed upon with admiration by a world at large.

The peculiarity of his appearance was in his countenance. His form had nothing remarkable. His frame was large and tall, his neck short. He was thin and spare in youth but grew corpulent in' maturer years. He was habited in his ordinary dress, a General's uniform; blue, faced with white, with one or two insignia of military orders on his breast. He occasionally came to the window of the palace, smiled and bowed to the crowds who came to greet him. With all the interest and veneration we feel in contemplating him, while we think he stands among the first, if not himself the first in policy and war; while all the praise due to his exalted genius shouldbe rendered; his wild, reckless and unrestrained ambition, spreads a cloud over the records of his glory, and does indeed "darken the splendor of victory:" so that while we admire the hero, we cannot love or approve the man.

The hundred days of his brief dominion were vari

Wlsly and actively spent in making preparations to tmeet the storm which from all parts of the political horizon was fast gathering round his devoted head. The declaration of war issued by the Allied Powers,-seemed wdl timed to call forth all the energies of his mighty mind, that as an Emperor he might meet the tlecisive day, and gather fresh laurels for France. Already the veterans of former fields were beginning to exult in the hope of new toils and new victories. When frequently reviewing his gathering troops, the expression of Parisian joy was reiterated. His princes, and marshals, and captains, renewing their vows of fidelity, were anxiously waiting the opportunity of signalizing their valor and skill more conspicuously than they had done in 1814.

On the first of June, the very splendid spectacle of the Champ de Mai was exhibited. Napoleon in his Imperial vestments, his chief officers in their state attire, attended by a large retinue of troops habited in all their variety of costume, passed before hundreds of thousands of Frerlch men, women and youths,-to witness an act of mutual loyalty and faith. A few days after, the Chief left the capital, and proceeded on to meet the decision of his fate at Waterloo.

The event of the battle is well known. Napoleon returned in defeat, and Paris was soon surrounded by the victorious armies. There was some fighting near the city, and numbers of waggons were employed in bringing in the wounded from the field. The flash and report of artillery were distinctly seen and heard from the streets; yet in the midst of all the danger so nigh, and all the anxiety they ought to have felt in the approaching crisis, the inhabitants were French-

men still. Business was attended to, recreation flourished; and with many the momentous circumstances without were little heeded. A number of the boys in the Lyceum, having heard that the Duke of Wellington had threatened to bombard the city from the heights of Montmartrie, unless a speedy entrance were granted, were disposed to be a little uneasy.

At length the city was surrendered; the king returned; and notwithstanding the rain which fell on the day of his grand entry, the ladies and gentlemen seemed to vie with each other in taking a commanding situation, from which to express their satisfaction at beholding his Majesty again. The fallen chief, appealing to the generosity of his conqueror, found the Prince Regent was influenced more by fear of the man, whose wars had drained so much English blood, than by a regard to his own glory in the estimation of the world.

During the occurrence of these important transactions, the writer was mostly within the limits of the school, but he well recollects seeing numbers of officers passing along the streets with an empty scabbard, having been deprived of their swords as a punishment for the feeling which could not brook the sudden blight of all their martial prospects in the establishment of Napoleon on the throne, while the nation was consigned, by a victory gained, and the subsequent residence of English troops dispersed through the country, to Bourbon weakness and superstition.

The duel was frequently resorted to, as the most expeditious way of settling disputes between such as mourned the defeat at Waterloo, and those that re i'oiced in the new change of government. After a little space for reflection, the vanquished party desisted from unavailing tumult,—perhaps because they had no master spirit to direct sedition— and order was measurably restored. While few but deprecated the barbarous policy that brought the young and brave Labedoyere to a traitor's death for standing in support of the Emperor's claim, less sympathy was awakened by the sentence of Marshal Ney, so often

deserting a falling cause entrusted to his fidelity.

A general admiration was felt at the courage of Madame La Vallette. Her husband had been arrested by the new government on a charge of treason, and sentenced to be shot. The night before his intended execution, his wife sought a last interview, which being granted, she clothed him in her own apparel, while she put on his male attire, and remained in prison in his stead. He escaped beyond the French dominions, and subsequently obtaining a pardon, he returned to his noble consort.

. CHAPTER VIII.

Mr. Colbum returns to London, and goes to Birmingham.—The Earl of Bristol proposes to patronize his son; he is placed at Westminster school.—Difficulty on account of fagging.

As already stated, Mr. Colbur n arrived in London with his son, in February, 1816. There never had been a time since they first left Cabot, that their pecuniary circumstances had been as low as they now were. Immediately on their arrival they called on Alderman Bridges, to make known their situation, and obtain information in regard to their present course and future prospects. But a few names had been obtained in support of the last undertaking, and the gentlemen concerned spake very discouragingly of the success of their scheme. It was evident that the committee had found it much easier to sit down, devise plans, and subscribe themselves, than it was to take hold like men of business, determined to pursue an energetic course and succeed.

Before long they expressed their inability to raise the proposed sum. The true reason probably was this: it was now nearly four years since Zerah Colburn first came to London; the unusual interest that was felt in his ease had now-much subsided, and at the present time, if any thing was effected, it must be done either by the liberality of a few, or by the persevering appeals of that few to the kindness of the public at large. Such liberality the few had not; such application to others was too laborious. While in Paris, being entirely dependent on the gifts or loans of friends, Mr. Colbur n felt his situation to be trying; but his son was provided for. It is true the officers of the Lyceum had frequently expressed a desire to have the initiatory sum of 750 francs paid; but it is at least probable that Zerah would never have been discharged from the school on account of this deficiency of means. Now these rich men, possessing ample means, and influence if disposed to employ it, had by their counsel, requests, and urging, removed his son from a school, where he was well provided for, and then forsook him without any cause, real or assigned, that could warrant them in such an ungentlemanly procedure. It is not strange that Mr. C. was at a loss what course to take in this critical juncture—without money, without friends, and ignorant of any art or calling by which to support himself in London.

Previous to his first visit to Paris, he had been invited by a Birmingham gentleman, Mr. Thomas Hadley, to bring his son to that place; but his intended journey to France rendered it inconvenient at that time. In the present dilemma a journey to Bir mingham was concluded upon.

When he arrived in that city Mr. Hadley recommended public exhibition as the proper way to introduce his case to the people. The patronage obtained jp this way was very limited,—a large part of the population being composed of mechanics and artizans, who had little interest or money to devote to objects of curiosity. Yet there were a number of persons who favored the American with very flattering attentions and kindnesses, and though unable to make splendid offers, they rendered the author's residence among them very pleasant and agreeable.

While in Birmingham a curious little incident took place; a Mr. Barker gave Zerah an invitation to call and dine at his house. This gentleman had an only child, a daughter six or seven years old: he told her who was coming to see them,.and described his calculating powers as something remarkably great. The child thought much upon it, and her meditation assumed such a turn, that when he came, she was afraid to enter the room where he was: she associated the idea of terror with that of wonderful, and probably thought that some being at least as bad as a ghost or a fiend was in the house. Her parents used every effort to explain the matter to her, but with many tears and sobs she persisted in keeping out of sight until he went away.

The system of Phrenology, first invented by Dr. Gall, was at that period beginning to prevail. A gentleman in Birmingham sought the opportunity of taking a cast in plaster of the upper part of Zerah'a face; as this process has already been alluded to and may not be generally understood, it will perhaps be satisfactory to some readers to have it more fully described. The materials used are Plaster of Paris, finely pulverized, and tepid water; being mixed into a thin composition, it is laid on the face with a spoon. It is sometimes customary to oil the hair, eyebrows, &c. to prevent adhesion, and to insert goose quills in the nostrils to afford a chance to breathe. The warmth of the face speedily dries the composition, when it is removed carefully, and-this mask serves as the mould for making the bust. Having tarried about three months in Birmingham, during whicj time Mr. Colbunf had visited London orice in order to try and incite the gentlemen to prosecute the object they had so lightly abandoned, without discovering any prospect of essential benefit, he concluded that it would be useless to remain there longer,.find resolved to remove his son to the metropolis, in order to continue his efforts to obtain patronage. For some time after their arrival they were in a very destitute condition, and debts were increasing for their necessary food. *At* length the idea suggested itself to his mind, of having his son confidentially explain his methods of calculation to such gentlemen as would become responsible for ten subscribers to the hook; one or two friends came into this arrangement, by which a relief for present exigencies was obtained.

In this state of uncertainty and poverty, matters went on, until July, 1816, when he called at the town residence of the Earl of Bristol, to ask his patronage on the above arrangement. The only acquaintance that he had previously had with his lordship, arose from his calling at Spring Gardens, while Zerah was exhibited, and leaving the names of himself and his two sons as subscribers for the memoir. In answer to his request, the Earl directed a note to him dated July 26th, stating that if Mr. C. would show the nature of his business he would appoint an hour for seeing him. Accordingly in another letter Mr. C. stated the object of the request more fully, and an interview was granted.

The reception which the father and his son received from the Earl was extremely gratifying. He manifested from the first a disposition to patronize the boy. He very patiently entered into the merits of the case, requesting a recital of all the circumstances which had transpired from the first discovery of his remarkable faculty, the plans which had been adopted for his patronage, and their respective failures. After obtaining what information Mr. Colburn could give, Jp.e expressed a wish to have his son go up to Putney heath, where his lordship usually resided at his country seat, during the summer months, and remain a few days, in order that the Earl might have a better opportunity of becoming acquainted with his habits, turn of mind, &c. before he made any definite proposals. He was justly anxious to ascertain the probability of his patronage being well bestowed, before he engaged very deeply in the subject.

Accordingly Zerah went to Putney, where the Duke of Norfolk, Lord Calthorpe, and Lord Templetown, were then on a visit. He received many expressions of kindness while there. The Earl had much conversation with him, in which he laid aside the reserve usually attendant upon rank, and with much afiability discoursed upon his progress in study, his gift of reckoning, and his views of religious truth. He was a scientific rather than a political man. He was not born to titles; in early life he held a captain's commission in the Navy, and by the death of the former Earl, Frederick William Hervey, being the nearest heir, exchanged his captain's berth and moderate pay for an Earl's coronet and the splendid estates of his childless predecessor.

He seldom took a prominent part in the discussions of the House of Peers, and while from his elevated rank he was doomed to participate in the fashionable pursuits of high life, as a good Churchman he was also anxious that the truths of revealed religion should be understood and believed by all. Though perhaps he might not have been fully acquainted with what we consider to be experimental piety, and of this we cannot satisfactorily judge, in all his intercourse and correspondence with the writer, he has manifested a. deep and parental solicitude for his usefulness in this world, and his happiness hereafter. He seemed particularly desirous to guard the mind of his youthful *protegi* from that Infidelity of sentiment which was common in the country he had recently left, and which was considerably prevalent in England. I9 reference to this, and well aware of the forcible manner in which the Bible proves itself, against all the attacks of skepticism, he enjoined upon him the task of committing to memory the fifty-third chapter of the Prophecy of Isaiah, for which he gave him a pound note.

After tarrying at Putney three or four days, Zerah returned to his father's lodgings in Somerstown, a village in the suburbs of London, being clad in a new suit of clothes, the gift of the Earl, with the understanding that he should hear more from his lordship.

Had this noble patron here limited his friendship, the author's obligations to him would have been great; but when it is remembered that these were only the first fruits of a liberality that continued eight years, the reader need not wonder that a pleasure is taken in describing them so minutely.

After the lapse of a week or ten days, a note was received from the Earl, requesting him to call again at Putney with his father. They went. His lordship then fully made known his intentions, viz.; to place the boy at Westminster

school; to keep him there until he should have completed his studies in that seminary, probably seven or eight years; to pay for his tuition, board, and other incidental expenses. He directed Mr. Colburn to go to the Institution, and ascertain the amount of the annual sum that would be necessary to answer all these demands. He also expressed his intention of furnishing Zerah with a number of books that he considered would be useful in establishing his religious views, viz. Bishop Butler's Analogy, Paley's Natural Theology and Horse Paulina?, Wilberforce's Practical View of Christianity, and Dr. Doddridge's three Sermons on the Evidences of Christianity, which were soon presented to him.

It now appeared to Mr. Colburn that better days were suddenly approaching, to compensate for the trials and disappointments which he had experienced, and both he and his son were highly encouraged. On application for a bill of expenses at Westminster school, it was ascertained that the whole amount would be about 140 pounds sterling (620 dollars). The Earl made arrangements with his banker to furnish this sum in half yearly payments to Mr. C. in order to meet the several annual terms of settlement required by the financial department of the school, and on the 19th September, he was regularly entered as a student there.

When the above named day came, he was taken along to the school, and delivered into the care of Dr. Page, the head master. This gentleman and Mr, Ellis, the head master of the lower school, took Zerah apart, (in the school room,) and spent a few minutes in examining into the progress he had made. Being quite Frenchified in his pronunciation of the Latin, and not at all familiar with the books used in that school, they placed him in the lowest class, and gave him a Latin Grammar, iEsop's Fables, &c.

As before intimated, the ancient languages were the only study pursued within this school: the manner of teaching was decidedly calculated to accustom the mind of the tyro to his task, and

render it easy and familiar. In the recitation of every lesson, the master required his class to parse every word of importance, and at the same time to repeat the rules verbatim for the government of the word. The failure of a word in repeating the rules in parsing, or in the previous exercise of construing the passage, rendered the scholar liable to be displaced by his more accurate comrade. The lessons were adapted to the ability of the student,—at first a few lines, not more than four or six, were given to translate, and bring in a writen copy thereof—and in the four years spent in the under school, fourteen or sixteen lines were not often exceeded. To prepare this lesson for construing and parsing, quoting all tbc rules connected therewith, was generally considered a sufficient task by the scholars—the little that was learnt at a time was by this course learnt thoroughly, and far more useful than if a longer lesson had been hurried over in a hasty and careless manner.

The first lesson on Monday morning was a recitation of the Church Catechism contained in the Common Prayer, (not the Westminster Catechism, though recited in Westminster) among the younger classes, while the older ones studied a higher work called the "Exposition of the Catechism;" The Masters and It was a prerogative vested in the hands of the tiro head masters to inflict the punishment of the rod, upon such scholars as were reported to them for that purpose by the assistant ushers.

Ushers were all ministers of the Church of England, and accordingly paid strict attention to this part of learning. The books used in the under school, during four years, were principally iEsop's Fables, Ovid'a Fasti, Cornelius Nepos, and a selection from the Metamorphoses. Two books, Clark's Introduction to making Latin, and a summary of Scripture History, were used for translating English into that language. Virgil, Caesar's Commentaries, &c. were not studied till admission into the upper-school, where the Greek Grammar was taken hold of.

The boys were summoned into

school an hour before breakfast; after which meal, they went in again at nine and continued till noon; and again from half past one till four o'clock. On every Tuesday, Thursday, and Saturday, there was no attendance required in the afternoon, and very frequently some great man would call in and request the head master to give his scholars leave to play during the remainder of the day, which request was uniformly granted. Added to all these, the festival of every saint mentioned in the calendar, was distinguished by services in the church and a cessation from study. Besides, the stated vacations at different periods of the year amounted to three months in all, so that in fact the true term appropriated to study could not much exceed seven months in the year. The discipline of the school was in aspect decided and strict, though not so in reality. The birch rod was the *ne plus ultra* of punishment in ordinary cases, beyond which expulsion (seldom resorted to) was enforced.

From the above named circumstances, it need not be a matter of surprise, that eight years should be required to obtain a knowledge of Latin and Greek; while the same term spent in the French Seminary, at less than one third of the annual expense, would send the student forth with a general-and excellent education.

The study of languages was generally pleasing to Zerah: little requiring the aid of a patiently investigating mind, which he never had, but depending principally on the exercise of the memory, he eagerly gave his attention to the French: the Latin was less charming in its outward aspect and construction, but it had its interest. It was a language of antiquity in which poets had sung, and historians had recorded the memorials of Roman fame and splendor, and presented to the mind a region worth exploring, and intellectual pleasures worthy of pursuit.

At the period of his entrance at Westminster school, he was a few days over twelve years old— quite old for the class in which he was placed, but for that reason better able, as well as by his eight months' attendance at the Lyceum

in Paris, to get speedily removed into a higher class. During the two years and nine months that he was connected with this institution, he accomplished the labor for which the boys generally spent four or five years. He learned with facility, and the continual practice preserved what he acquired fresh in his memory. It is, however, a truth which may as well be stated here as any where else, that the mind of Zerah was never apparently endowed with such a talent for close thinking on intricate subjects as many possess. He was not peculiarly fortunate in arriving at a result which did not readily present itself, or for which the process leading thereto was not soon discovered. It is for this reason that he has been unable to discover a prospect of his extensive usefulness in mathematical studies, or of justifying the high expectations which many had reasonably formed on account of his early endowment, and hence he feels more reconciled than he otherwise might in abandoning the wisdom and literature of this world for the duties of his present important calling. While in school he generally sustained himself among the four at the head of the class; but was not remarkable either for quickness of mind or closeness of application.

Among the customs peculiar to Westminster school, was the performing bf Latin plays just before the commencement of the Christmas vacation. The comedies of Terence were selected for this purpose; and the several characters were sustained by the members of the higher classes; the audience consisted chiefly of the other scholars.

The commencement of the season of *Lent* was signalized by a peculiar ceremony; as among the Catholics, so the Protestant Church recognizes this period of abstinence, though it is not observed with the same rigor and austerities. On Shrove-Tuesday, at noon, the scholars and teachers being on the point of quitting the school room, the cook of St. Peter's College is ushered in, bearing in his hand a frying pan with a pancake just cooked; after paying his salutations to the audience, he proceeds to show his dexterity by throwing the cake

over the iron bar that was extended across the upper part of the room, about twenty feet high, and the scholar who was so dexterous as to catch it, had it for his pains. The origin of this custom is unknown.

The custom-of fagging has already been alluded to. After Zerah had spent the first three weeks in becoming domesticated to the establishment, he was informed that he must commence his menial occupations, and a boy in the upper school pitched upon him to be his waiter. In addition to what has been said relative to washing dishes, cleaning boots and shoes, &c. it may be proper to state more fully that the boarding houses provided breakfast, dinner, and a late supper at eight in the evening. The gentlemen of the upper school generally provided themselves with a supply of dishes for setting their tea table at five o'clock, and it was to furnish this meal that a part of the fag's labor was required.

It so happened one Friday night, the first or second week that he commenced his services, that having been dismissed by his regular master, another called on him to do some work. He did it in such a manner that his master, the son of a baronet, Sir John L. Kaye, was very much displeased, and as a righteous castigation, took his left hand, twisted round the arm as far as he could, and then with clenched fist proceeded deliberately to beat his shoulder black and blue. He was a full-grown lad, eighteen years old, and in addition to his size, it was a decree among the students that any member of the under school lifting his hand against one of the upper school, should receive "wrath without mixture," the award of their combined and summary vengeance. This was too much like the treatment of the poor and degraded African, whose wrongs are day and night crying unto God for deliverance, and who, should he dare to lift his hand to guard his person from the lawless arm of the white man's tyranny, must die. And this is justice! this is liberty! If there be in all the magazines of Divine wrath a bolt more heavy, a storm of impending retribution more terrible than the rest, may we not expect it will yet fall in all its fury to punish us as a Nation for this abomination of our brethren.

The next day Zerah went home to his father, related what had happened, and showed his wounds and bruises. His father was very much surprised and displeased, and being a man of very independent feelings soon made up his mind that matters should not go on in this manner. Accoidingly when his son went back on Sunday evening, he accompanied him, and called upon Mr. Knox, the usher who was stationed in charge of the boarding-house where he boarded. On learning the circumstances of the case, Mr. Knox manifested a good deal of regret at the abuse that Zerah had received; when Mr. Colburn made known his dissatisfaction at the custom of fagging, from which all this had proceeded, and his resolution to have his son a fag no longer, Mr. K. expressed his opinion that he could not be liberated from this service. Mr. C. told him very frankly that he did not place his son there to be a servant, but to study.

Mr. Knox appealed to the antiquity of the custom, that for more than a hundred years it had prevailed there and in the other public seminaries of the kingdom; a custom which many fathers had attempted to evade in favor of their children without success. Mr Colburn, he said, had better remove his son, if the practices and usages of the school were disagreeable to him. To this a prompt reply was given: "if you have power to expel my son for not fagging, you may; I shall not take him away, neither shall he be a fag."

It appeared from Mr. Knox's conversation and deportment that he deemed it most for the interest of the school to persevere in a course that would not disaffect, in the persons of their sons, the rich and titled patrons of the establishment, by taking away their waiters. As Mr. Colburn obtained nothing satisfactory from him, he left his son with a promise to return on Tuesday morning and see how matters proceeded, charging him at the same time to do nothing for any of his seniors in the interim.

The next day it was rumored round that some trouble was gathering; the scholars made up their minds to repel the attempted innovation on their privileges. By some means Zerah managed to evade his masters during the day, but in the evening, under the same roof where Mr. Knox was engaged in his study, a number of the largest boys got him into their midst, and ordered him to work; the job required was to clean a pair of shoes, (if he remembers aright;) he refused, stating as one reason the command of his father; they threatened; still he remained obstinate: finally they proceeded from words to blows, and laid on without mercy, until he complied with their requirement.

The next morning by sunrise, his father arrived and made inquiries as to his situation; Zerah told him what had happened, and his father called on Mr. Knox, but was treated with perfect contempt. He then started to go over to see Dr. Page the head master; on his way the boys from the windows hooted and yelled at the "Yankee." Dr. Page's view of the subject was similar to that of the usher: he stated his inability to abrogate the custom, but if Mr. Colburn desired it, he was ready to expel Kaye for the abuse of his son. Mr. Colburn said he did not wish to have the young man expelled, but that he should be taught to behave himself more like a scholar. Said he, "when I placed my son under your care, I did it in confidence that as a father you would watch over, govern, and protect him he also told the Doctor tfiat if the officers of the school did not do their duty, he should take the protection of his son into his own hands and defend him by the law of Nature. Finding him resolute in his purpose, Doctor Page and Mr. Knox had a consultation, the event of which was that in the forenoon, as Mr. Colburn was walking towards the boarding house, Mr. K. sent out his servant with a note; remembering his supercilious conduct, Mr. C. threw it away unopened. Mr. Knox then came out himself, made such concessions as were accepted, and finally assured him that his son should not be compelled to fag any more; satisfied

with this arrangement, Mr. Colburn gladly left his son and returned home.

The manner in which the custom of fagging first arose and grew into its present strength and permanent existence is not known; but the patronage it receives is a blot and reproach upon English fathers. The universality of its impartial power, favoring the son of a Duke or Earl no more than the son of a poor It is an affair of no small moment to be expelled from one of the public seminaries, as it excludes from the Universities, and from all the patronage flowing thence, whether in the Church, the Army,. or Navy. It is a severe disgrace. mechanic, affords no vindication of its oppressions. With little exception it has been assented to and allowed by all parents who had placed their children at a public institution, though a few instances have occurred of their removal, rather than have them subjected to such unjustifiable abuse. We are not aware of any moral or intellectual pleasure or advantage that is secured by its perpetuity, any further than to gratify that desire so prevalent in many young minds to amuse themselves by the sufferings of others. Every feeling of the virtuous mind calls loudly for its destruction. When that period will comeTio one can know. CHAPTER IX.

Remarks upon Mr. Colburn's situation. —Zerah goes to spend his vacations with the RevMr. Bullen.—He leaves Westminster school.

The inquiry has without doubt already suggested itself to the mind of the reader, in what way Mr. Colburn supported himself while in London. That while at home with his family, he was a hard work. ing man, appears from a certificate to that purpose sent to him by the selectmen of Cabot, in 1811, as well as from the present testimony of his family and others who knew him well. But it was true, and need excite little surprise, that having a son so peculiarly endowed by his Creator, and so many advisers, who were sure that they could point out through the medium of this gift tlie direct road to celebrity and wealth, he learned to rely more than was safe upon external appearances for his support.

On his first arrival in London, in 1812, when the public mind was unanimously excited in hi favor, wishing to be directed to some employment by which to support himself that he might not be an unnecessary burthen upon the patronage his son received, his friends discouraged the idea, assuring him of a readiness and ability on their part to take care of both the father and the son. During the time that hiS child had been exhibited, it was necessary that he should be accompanied by some suitable guardian and protector; his father discharged that office faithfully.

Since the close of his public exhibition, he had been still engaged in following those gentlemen who had undertaken to patronize, in order to assist in accomplishing their intentions. The time had never yet arrived, when he could see his son so well provided for as to justify him in leaving him, to return to America. At the present, he was very desirous of having the contemplated memoir published, that the expectations of subscribers might be answered, and himself realize some pecuniary advantage therefrom. Soon after his son was established at Westminster, a new Prospectus was drawn up, by whom is not recollected, stating, doubtless for the encouragement of subscribers, what was absolutely unfounded, that the book was in the press, when as yet not a line of manuscript had been prepared.

The gentlemen on the original committee had selected a person of mathematical reputation at Woolwich to write, and he had all the papers and documents in his possession two or three years. He returned them without using. Mr. Colburn afterwards placed them in the hands of a gentleman of the Inner Temple, but he also laid them in a safe place for years longer, and returned them in the same condition. Had he been able to reconcile his mind to leave his son, when established at Westminster, and bequeath the memoir to Mr. Montagu and his associates, to publish when they should have obtained from Biggs the amount of his delinquencies, and returned home, though the separa-

tion would have been extremely unpleasant to his son, yet it would undoubtedly have been for the best. This however he did not do.

In London he could not pursue any trade, having neither the means, nor the necessary apprenticeship of seven years, and in the farming sections, he could have succeeded no farther than to work as a day laborer; and it may be, that having much republican feeling, and high expectations, his mind shrunk from such a state of dependance as an English daylaborer is subjected to. Yet after all, it is probable 9 that even a day-laborer's life would have yielded more certain profit, and if he were contented therein, more happiness, than the course he pursued. About this time, he forwarded some Prospectuses to this country, for the purpose of obtaining subscribers for the book, but none were obtained.

His son being now settled in a course of study, for some time his father subsisted upon such occasional donations as persons who had been concerned in former plans were pleased to contribute; but this course, however justifiable it might have been on the ground of their previous undertakings and plans, which had failed for want of their perseverance, was irksome and revolting, or ought to have been, to his mind; and besides, more than all these contributions was actually requisite in order that he might be comfortably maintained.

At last the idea occurred to him that by removing his son from his situation as a whole boarder at Westminster, and having him board a part of the time at home, he might be personally profited by the bounty of Lord Bristol. There were many students attending school in this manner: lodging at their parents' houses, and receiving breakfast and dinner at the boarding house. So long as this alteration secured his son's opportunities for study and improvement equally with the other arrangement, he deemed it most advisable, and at the time, the Earl expressed no disapprobation at the change. Perhaps the Earl was unacquainted with it, yet the writer believes he was informed of it.

Sometime afterwards, in the summer of 1817, being still attentive to the interest of his charge, he made provision for the boy to spend his terms of vacation in the family of a clergyman, Rev. Henry St. John Bullen, his Lordship's chaplain, for the express purpose, as stated in one of his letters, "of placing him in a situation to acquire other attainments, which, though-less essential than morals and learning, were nevertheless not to be neglected." Thus a plan seemed to be well formed and fully matured for preparing him in all respects for literary, scientific and polished society; and having now done every thing that appeared necessary to secure his welfare,. the Earl soon after set out with his wife and children, and their necessary attendants, to visit the continent of Europe.

There are in England few among that class whose means are adequate to the undertaking, that are insensible to the opportunities afforded for general information by traveling among the European nations: France, Germany, Switzerland, Italy, are explored; the Mediterranean sea, the Holy Land, with all its antiquities interesting to the man of science, or the Christian philosopher, are visited, and it generally happens that the traveler returns to his native land more attached to his country, its government and customs. This is indeed a natural consequence r not merely would they prefer England because it is their native land, but also on account of the decided superiority of its institutions, its civil, political, and religious privileges, above those of any nation on the continent. Lord Bristol, who at this time went principally for the benefit of his children, was absent nearly five years.

The Rev. Mr. Bullen, with whom the author now became acquainted, was a man in many respects well qualified for the task assigned. He had been educated at Cambridge, and for a number of years had been head Master of a Grammar school at Bury St. Edmund's, while formerly holding another living in the gift of the Earl. His literary acquirements, as might be expected, were very good, and his ministerial talents such as rendered Kim acceptable in the parish of Danton, Buckinghamshire, about forty miles from the capital, to which he had been removed.

JJeing much at leisure, and having no children, he undertook the private instruction of four boys in Latin and other branches. While residing with him, Zerah pursued his classical studies, and also surveyed the first six books of Simson's Euclid. Many have inquired if the study of Geometry was easy to him 1 He never found, that he recollects, any difficulty in understanding the demonstrations laid down by Euclid. Their fitness and adaptation to the various problems or theorems were very evident to his mind, but the study was always dry and devoid of interest. The reason probably was, that while studying he did not realize, even in anticipation, the benefits of such a science; had he been engaged in some pursuit that would have required the continual introduction and application of Geometrical principles, the subject would have assumed an interesting appearance, his mirid would have been engaged in it, and he would have remembered the principles and arguments laid down.

Mr. Bullen was occasionally in a mood of anecdote, and he had a numerous variety laid up in his head. He used to relate one in regard to the reason that his father had designed him for the church. When a little boy, he continually frequented a neighboring cabinet maker's shop, and often brought home square and triangular remnants of mahogany that were useless, and setting them up on the table or floor, would call them *his pulpit:* hence his father took the hint, sent him to school, then to college, and he was in due time admitted to orders. Whether he knew aught of evangelical regeneration, or had ever felt a divine conviction leading him to devote himself to the work of the ministry, is another point, on which we feel incompetent to decide.

To an individual confined from year to year in the tumult and bustle of London, the plan of spending a month or two during the pleasant season in the country was very agreeable, and it afforded some little opportunity of observing the difference between a cky 0 and a country life. The parish of Dunton was small, mostly lying at a little distance from the great roads, quite retired from the noise and hurry of any thing like a large population. The amount of tithes was something like" 150 pounds, or 666 dollars, besides the lands attached to the Parsonage.

The inhabitants of the parish were generally poor, but in number sufficient to fill for the most part the ancient stone church respectably on the Sabbath. There were but four farmers in the parish in independent circumstances; the-rest were employed in laboring by the day; yet they appeared to enjoy themselves. It is not recollected that any school existed in the place for the instruction of their children. At no greater distance than this from London, the corruption of the English, or rather the traces of a former, dialect have been observed, in the use of words entirely new, provincial, and unintelligible. It is a circumstance of some little curiosity, that while in our vast territory one language will generally answer the purpose of him who travels from one extremity to another, on that little island there are so many varieties of dialect, differing so much from each other; and it seems to be a striking comment on their poverty, their lack of means for information, and the few facilities they have for corresponding with each other from north to south, or from east to west.

The produce of their farms consists of grass, and of wheat, rye, barley, and oats, for grain: very little bread is made of any grain beside wheat; sometimes rye is used, or barley. The great demand for barley is at the brew-houses for making malt.» No Indian corn is raised in that country, unless William Cobbett has carried home the secret from this. While in France, the writer visited at the country seat of an American gentleman,'where corn, roasted and boiled, was presented in good order for eating.

Their seasons are more temperate than ours; it is seldom that the snows come to any great depth, and they speedily melt away. During some winters in London, there would not be a flake visible until the middle of January, and then perhaps two or three light storms of half an inch or an Inch, melted almost as soon as fallen: very seldom it lies for several days. The weather is generally warm in summer, so as to be delightfully pleasant; yet such is the inconstancy of the climate, that a sultry day may be followed by a frosty night.

Some travelers have formed an idea that a clear sky is hardly ever seen from the island of Great Britain, on account of everlasting fogs. The writer can honestly give it as his opinion that he saw the clear blue ethereal a great many times while he staid in Europe, and he certainly thought it must be the sky; he cannot conceive what else should have that cerulean appearance above. The fall and part of the winter are the term prescribed by law for hunting and shooting. From the first of September to the fourteenth of February, those who are qualified by possessing a certain amount of property, and have purchased the license annually granted, may kill partridges, pheasants, hares, &c. with guns or dogs. If other persons, or those qualified at other times, kill game, and thus violate the ancient feudal law, they are liable to prosecution and fines.

Hunting the fox or the stag, (which last are generally kept in gentlemen's parks to be turned out when sport is desired) forms a great diversion for the higher classes, notwithstanding the dangers which attend it, and the injury thence accruing to the farming community. Forty or more men mounted on horses of the English hunter breed, and occasionally a lady in the train, with as many dogs disciplined to the business, will follow the fox or stag across roads, fences, ditches, fields of standing grain or grass, at the hazard of their necks. Ten, twenty, and even thirty miles are sometimes traveled in this style of Jehu-driving, without any stop or interruption, until the panting, exhausted object of their pursuit, is overtaken and slain. Almost every farmer keeps a couple of greyhounds, for the purpose of coursing hares, to feast upon himself, or to send to his friends in the city.

The residence of the writer at Mr. Bullen's was very agreeable in a number of respects. He was a man of many eccentricities, however, and some of them not at all pleasing; he did not seem to possess all the patience that was requisite for an instructer of youth; and in some instances, through hastiness of temper, treated him with harshness and injustice, whereby the perfect satisfaction he would have felt at being under his roof was much diminished. Providence had favored him in the person of his wife, with one of the best of her sex, and she occasionally suffered a little in her feelings from the exuberance of his. As far as country air, opportunity for learning, and access to a library, which though small in England would be considered large by our people, were desirable objects, in a pleasant and retired situation, Dunton was a very eligible place.

After having spent the vacations of two years at Mr. Bullen's, Zerah was informed by his tutor that the Earl of Bristol had an intention of removing him from Westminster, and of placing him wholly under Mr. B.'s direction. As this idea was perfectly new to Zerah, so it was to his father, when the clergyman wrote to him, giving information of the contemplated change. Undoubtedly the benevolent nobleman had a right to dispense his charity in the way that pleased him best, and to say that he would no longer support the boy unless removed from Westminster school; but from the uniform condescension and kindness with which he had hitherto treated Mr. Colburn, it seemed no more than likely that he would first have consulted the parent's feelings in relatjon to the change, if the design had been his own: Mr. C. therefore concluded that the step was first suggested by Mr. B. with a view to his own personal emolument.

The Earl was a,t that time as far off as Spa, in Germany, and all the knowledge he could have on the subject was probably derived from the representations of one, and that one perhaps personally interested. It would have been quite an addition to the Rector's moderate stipend, if he had contrived to secure the annual sum paid at Westminster for the board and tuition of Zerah. On receiving his letter Mr. Colburn immediately went down to see him; he tarried two days at Dunton, and formed such an opinion of the clergyman, whether well-founded or not, as fixed him in the determination not to place his son under his care. The author would observe that however much he respected his tutor for his ministerial character and literary qualifications, two or three months in the year, were as much as he should have been willing to spend under his care.

Returning to London, his father wrote immediately to the Earl, stating the matter according to the light in which it appeared to him; in his reply his lordship appeared decided to have the boy established in a course different from his present one, but at the same time, kindly offered, if Mr.-C. would let his son stay a year with Mr. Bullen, to allow him £50 for his own support. Had his father seen fit to come into this arrangement, though no way agreeable to the feelings of Zerah, it is probable that his education would have progressed; and perhaps at the expiration of the year, some different arrangement would have been entered into, mutually satisfactory-to all the parties concerned. This, however, he would not do, and consequently in May, 1819, he left the school.

Thus withdrawing from the patronage of the man who alone had undertaken to do all for him that his case required, let the writer be permitted to express bis regret that any thing should have occurred, carrying in its aspect the bare insinuation that the object of his kindness undervalued its sincerity and extent. It falls to the lot of very few to meet with such a friend: therefore it seems doubly a duty that such friendship should be appreciated—to return it is, in the very nature of things, impossible.

Mr. Colburn always retained a lively sense of the benevolence of his noble Patron, but it may appear to some that he ought at all events to have entered into the arrangement devised above. His son feels assured that his father acted in this matter according to what he deemed a correct principle; he also feels unable to say which course was actually for the best: but it seems as if with so much patronage offered by a man who was able and willing to assist,#some plan ought to have been acceded to that would have shown more fully the grateful sense entertained, and the high value set upon such patronage. May the Lord repay that noble spirited gentleman here and hereafter!

CHAPTER X.

Mr. Colburn suggests the Stage to his son.—Remarks upon Theatres.—He commences Actor.—Goes to Edinburgh and Glasgow.— Dugald Stewart.— Visits Ireland, and returns to London.

Having now no longer any definite plan devised; being favored with the counsels of no one who might prescribe the most advantageous course, but being left to his own resourses, to decide upon some means whereby he might make the talent of his son profitable, Mr. lolburn was for some time in ignorance as to any thing that promised even the appearance of success. Zerah was now in his fifteenth year; his education was in a very unfinished state, so that there seemed to be no way in which he could turn his natural or acquired abilities to good account, in promoting the object which his friends had long entertained.

After much thought and anxiety on the point, it occurred to his mind that there was one calling for which he thought his son had a taste, in which he had not yet been engaged, and which might be productive of pecuniary advantage, namely, the Stage. He proposed it to his son, and he, being young and having a fondness for display, was well pleased with the foolish notion. While young he had imbibed an idea probably common to young minds, that there was quite a dignity and honor attached to their characters who personated Kings, Emperors, Patriots, and other great men: that it was very noble to spout forth their lofty sayings, and to show a large applauding audience how natural it was to represent such exalted personages.

The next point to be ascertained was whether the young calculator had any original gift or qualification for such an avocation. The proprietor of Covent Garden Theatre, was applied to for his opinion, and he thought there was much-"probability of succes according-ly he furnished him with a ticket of free admission to the Theatre, in order that by seeing others perform, he might gain more insight into the mysteries of the drama. A teacher was engaged to. hear him recite his speeches, another to in-struct him in handling the sword; had he been at home employed in the labo-rious pursuits of the farmer, how much more honorable it would have appeared. Well knowing that his father had always entertained a poor opinion of the gener-al reputation of the stage, his son was much surprised when he first mentioned to him this project: he made no objec-tion, however. He can account for the adoption of this scheme by his father, only on the principle of necessity to hit upon some expedient to get a living; his father designed to accompany him; and it is beyond a doubt in his own mind that had he continued in this way of life, he would always have enjoyed parental influence and caution to preserve him from the immoralities that are so com-mon among that profession.

For the present, therefore, the idea of acquiring an Education was superseded. The effect produced upon his friends and advisers by the new movement, was such as might have been anticipated. They could not think that it was in this path that he was destined to rise to hon-orable fame, and they doubted the pro-priety of his devoting himself to such a work: they used their best arguments to dissuade him from it, but the fact was, something must be done, and this seemed as likely to succeed as any other undertaking.

The dramatic tutor at first engaged was dismissed, and Mr. Charles Kem-ble, one of the principal ac tors at Covent Garden, was applied to; he un-dertook the task, and for two or three montjis the boy waited upon his instruc-tions.

At that period the stage was not held in such poor repute as it now is in this country. There were in London fourteen play houses, which were well filled Jpry night. Some of the actors engaged re-ceived eighty or a hundred dollars per week, while all who had but middling qualifications were able to support themselves. The character of the drama was high; many looked up to it as the source from which their purest notions of virtue were to proceed. This senti-ment, if it ever had any foundation in truth, seems entirely unsupported at the present day. While indeed we are ready to admit that there are many truths of the most elevated character contained in some plays; while we would not with-hold the tribute of applause that is due to the talents o£ some dramatic writers, for the correct representation they give of human nature in all its variety of good and evil tendencies, still we think it will be the unqualified expression of evey ingenuous mind which is informed on the subject, that exhibitions which so frequently present to the mind the idea of almost every vice or crime to which man is liable, cannot exert a very salu-tary influence upon the moral or reli-gious state of the community.

Should it be said that the inhabitants of ancient Lacedemon acted on a similar principle, in making their slaves intoxi-cated, and then exhibiting them to their children in order to excite in their minds a greater abhorrence of drunkenness, we think it may with propriety be replied, that degenerate man, unless endowed with a larger measure of divine grace than usually prevails over a theatrical audience, will be more prone to imbibe, imitate, and obey the unholy example which flits before his eyes, and insinu-ates itself into his soul, than to reject it. Should it still he urged that the moral in-fluence of the stage is not in presenting every form of sin, but in setting forth its punishment upon the guilty, and thus vindicating insulted, suffering virtue, we would say it seems inefficient after the chain is thrown around, and the fet-ter is riveted on the captive, to under-take to rescue.

Perhaps indeed the crime of suicide, by which so many dramatic heroes end a virtuous life, amid tflk shouts of Christians, applauding their elevation ana fortitude of character, thus becomes less repulsive in its nature, and renders the disappointed, the dishonored, or the suffering, more reckless of the conse-quences of such an act, and indirectly leads them to its perpetration. What else could be expected from a place where the doctrines of the Gospel are seldom or never mentioned, and the morality of the Bible would be thought out of place. The ungentlemanly profaneness which is so bountifully introduced in their comic prod 'ctions, may suit the vulgar ear, but cannot nourish the germ of any virtue in the souL The advocates of Anti-Masonry, who among many ob-jections to the Masonic system, urge as an important one, the profanation of the Christian religion, would do well to as-certain whether the frequent use and in-troduction of religious forms on the stage, before assembled thousands, is not calculated to be as great a curse to the nation, as the supposed transactions within the Lodge: especially if they en-courage the drama. Added to which, the glaring immodesty which characterizes some of their performances, must be re-volting in the extreme to every mind of refined and delicate feeling, not to say, of Christian propriety and reserve.

And who are they that stand at the threshold of this school of correct prin-ciples who are they that minister around this altar, whose kindling incense is thought to purify by its fires, illuminate by its brilliancy, and refresh by its fra-grance 1 We do not say that no actor is as exemplary and amiable in private life, as he is applauded in his public ca-reer; but such characters are rare; the greater part, even of the actresses, are persons whose reputation has been sul-lied, not wholly by the breath of calum-ny. So much so, that they could not be considered fit companions in a discreet and virtuous circle.

While such is the case in that part of the house propriated to the actors, the other divisions, devoted to the ac-commodation of spectators, are in per-fect keeping. Instead of finding, as some might anticipate, in every waiter a servant of true philosophy, in every sur-rounding guest a bosom fired with the thirst of wisdom, and goodness, he will find intoxicating liquors presented: tip-plers, pickpockets and sharpers, contin-ually suggesting the need of a double guard, not only upon his principles, but also upon his purse; and where his in-experienced mind migh t imagine the fairy forms continually passing, as the handmaids of the palace of Wisdom, he sees abandoned females, lost to every consciousness of forgotten purity, with all their alluring arts and blandishments, shameless in crime, and boundless in ef-frontery, who are engaged— shall we say in fastening upon the mind the good impressions already received?—No; but with all the combined power of precept and example, soliciting to unholy indul-gence; and there is but a narrow chance for the unpractised frequenter of such places to return unwounded and entire.

Should the serious reader here in-quire if with such views of the nature and tendency of the stage, the writer consented to be a play-actor, he truly answers, no; though at that time he was not particularly influenced by consider-ations of a religious sort. Yet he should have shrunk from a course thus dis-played to his mind: he was then very young; little acquainted with the evils it entailed on many; and on the whole considered that calling as eligible as any other. It has been by subsequent ac-quaintance and observation that he has been led to a more correct and estab-lished view of the subject. If there be any part of his life on which he is dis-posed to look with peculiar regret as wasted, while the whole has accom-plished little, it would be the year that was spent in preparing for the Theatre.

His first appearance in public was in the month of August, at Margate, a town seventy miles from Lon» don, which derived its principal consequence from being on the sea coast, and a place much frequented in the summer by persons who were anxious to escape from the confinement of the city, and enjoy the fresh air and salt-water bathing. The part he attempted was that of Norval, in Home's tragedy of Douglas; his first re-ception was tolarably flattering, but as the audiences were not very numerous, the receipts of the house were not suf-ficient to enable the proprietor to make him any compensation. After spending four weeks in Margate, he went back to London, about the first of September.

Having formerly visited Ireland and Scotland, Mr. Colburn thought it might serve his present interest to visit these countries again. Accordingly they packed up their scanty wardrobe, both common and theatrical, and embarked for Edinburgh on the 23d of the month. The distance by land is about four hun-dred miles; by sea, it is estimated to be four hundred and fifty. Their means were so limited that they had to engage a passage in the steerage, and after five days of hard fare they landed at Leith, the sea port, distant about one mile from the city of Edinburgh.

Here Mr. Colburn called upon a num-ber of his former friends, and as he was in a destitute situation, they contributed to his present wants. It did not however appear probable that he would receive any encouragement at the Theatre, and therefore after a short tarry, they left for Glasgow.

On their way to that city, they pro-ceeded by the steam-boat up the Frith of Forth about twenty miles, and then went overland three miles, to take passage in the canal boat which carried them to Glasgow. They went about two miles out of their way in order to call at Kin-neil House, the residence of Dugald Ste-wart. This celebrated man was then bending under the weight of infirmities, but he entertained them with hospitality and kindness while they staid, about an hour, when they regained the road which led to the canal, and arrived the next day at their place of destination.

Glasgow was not then what it had been to them on their former visit; of their friends, some were gone and some were estranged. Kirkman Finlay, of the Book Committee, probably thought that he had done enough by lending Mr. Colburn a hundred pounds in 1815, and took no present interest in his affairs. The prospect of patronage in theatricals, was as small as it had been in Edin-burgh, and they soon sailed for Belfast, in Ireland. As it had been six years be-fore, so now their reception in this town was very agreeable. Nearly all their for-mer acquaintances were still living, and manifested a sympathy for them in pro-moting the object of their present under-taking.

They engaged lodgings in the house of a Catholic family, and soon called on Mr. Talbot, the manager of the the-atre there. The dramatic company being then about to remove for a short recess to Londonderry, it was not deemed ex-pedient to introduce the young Ameri-can before the public previous to their return to Belfast. The interval was spent on expense, and. without any benefit. At length the strolling company started for Londonderry, and the new candidate for theatrical distinction followed them. Being scantily provided with cash, and having time at command, Mr. Colburn and Zerah set out on foot to travel a dis-tance of seventy miles.

It was in the winter season, and the weather was quite rainy on their jour-ney; they had, therefore, no favorable opportunity for observing the country through which they passed. A number of linen manufactories lay on their road, and they saw pieces of their manufac-ture bleaching on the grass. The snow had not begun to fall. After being out three nights, they arrived at Londonder-ry. Before they came in sight of the town they saw numbers of carts at the peat bogs, receiving their loads, which were transported to the doors of such as wished to purchase fuel, but were too poor to buy coal. The town i» entered by crossing a long bridge built of timber, and furnished at one end with a draw-bridge for the accommodation of ves-sels that wish to pass up the river, be-ing the only bridge constructed of that material which the writer remembers to have seen on the other side of the At-lantic. This city is surrounded by a wall nearly a mile in length, twelve or fifteen feet high, and as many in widjn, and is remarkable on account of the siege it sustained against the Catholic king James the Second, in 1688. They still celebrate as a public festival the 18th of

February, the anniversary of their deliverance.

Zerah Colburn had no opportunity afforded him of appearing before the citizens of that place in any character that was congenial to his taste; the loftiness of the tragic muse suited him much better than the comic department: but the term of their petformance there having expired, the company made arrangements for returning to Belfast. While here he received the most singular caution, considering by whom it was given, that he ever received. The manager, Talbot, was a man who, on very slight provocation, and sometimes on none at all, would break out into excessive and horrid profanity. One night while dressing for the stage, some trifle disconcerted him: as usual, he poured forth a torrent of execrations and oaths; the writer was standing near him. Talbot suddenly stopped, and fixing his eye keenly upon him, "Colburn," said he, "take care that you neuer suffer yourself to get into a habit of swearing; if you do, it will be impossible for you to overcome it." Poor slave!

Having returned to Belfast, preparations speedily commenced for their spring campaign: and in a week or two the young arithmetician was introduced on the boards in the part of King Richard the Third; on a subsequent occasion he appeared as Lothair, in the tragedy called Adelgitha. But either Theatricals were at too low an ebb in that place, or his talents for that profession (if he had any) were not sufficiently matured to render his continued residence in Belfast profitable.

As already stated, the author lodged in the house with a Catholic family; the lady of the house, a widow, and her three daughters, were well established in the doctrines of the church of Rome, and faithfully observed every Friday and Saturday as days of abstinence from flesh. A short time before his departure, the fast of Lent commenced; this fast is observed, though with different degrees of rigor, both in the Protestant and Catholic churches, in memory of the Saviour's fasting forty days in the wilderness. The night before it commenced, having gone to bed, he was waked up between eleven and twelve, by the young women of the house with a plate full of bacon and eggs, and he was urged to eat. the case was this: anticipating a long term of abstinence from any meat except fish, they were sitting up partaking till the last moment, of the good things that would be soon interdicted by their church.

About the first of April, 1820, Zerah left Belfast for the city of Dublin, a distance of eighty Irish, or one hundred and ten English miles. The journey was cheered by accounts of sundry robberies that had been and still were attempted of the Mail Coach, but they arrived without any disturbance of this nature.

Mr. Harris, the proprietor of Covent Garden Theatre, was then in Dublin, fixing up the *Rotunda* building for a temporary theatre, until a more-permanent establishment could be erected; Mr. Colburn applied to him for employment; but without success. It wan while here, that the writer commenced his attempts at dramatic composition. Hoole's translation of "Jerusalem Delivered," was adopted, to furnish the plot of a Tragedy; but it never had any merit, or any success.

It was here also that an opportunity presented itself for an interview with that very eccentric character, the Reverend Charles R. Maturin, author of several gloomy plays and novels; he officiated in one of the Protestant churches in Dublin, but as a preacher his talents were not remarkable. In addition to his literary fame, he had the reputation of being one of the best dancers of the day.

The first of May would bave passed with as little notice as many other days, had it not been, that some little bustle more than usual was observed. On looking more closely, something like a procession of rude peasants was seen, and on inquiry it was ascertained that this was the day for celebrating the potato plant, specimens of the present year's growth being carried round.

Much of the time since the writer left Westminster school, had been passed in comparative unhappiness. Not only at times scantily supplied with the necessaries of life, but also a victim to that oppressive feeling which rises up in the moments of inactivity and sloth, from having no employment to pursue, and which spreads its disheartening influence all over the mind. Of all lives, it would seem that his is most ignoble and joyless, who has nothing to do with or for himself, in using the talents committed to his charge. Frequently walking down to the wharf, or the beach, and beholding vessels whose sails were filling to the breeze, bound for an American port, his heart would become sad, and burn with desire to be on the way to his native land.

After tarrying in Dublin about four months, he made preparation to go to London. For this purpose A he embarked on the 11th of July in a packet sloop bound to Liverpool, the distance being estimated at one hundred and twenty miles. An opportunty now presented itself for learning a new trait in the character of the poor Irish—(heir improvidence. On the deck of the vessel were collected about two hundred and fifty poor fellows, from different sections of the country, who were going over to England to obtain work during the hay and harvest season, in order to earn some cash wherewith to pay their rents at home, &c. Of this large number, a small part only had furnished themselves with a sufficient quantity of provisions to last them till they landed at Liverpool; some had enough for a day or two; while the larger proportion actually sailed with just nothing at all in their wallets, that was made to eat: just so void of thought were they.

During the first two nights, the weather was very mild and serene; the two last of the passage were considerably windy. The poor Irishmen were quite alarmed, and began to think it was time to call some good saint to their aid. At every heaving of the vessel, they all muttered over their prayers in a low tone of voice, as if expecting it would soon be all over with them. Sunday morning came; the vessel lay off near the island of Anglesea, on the Welch coast. It was now the third day that some of them had had nothing to eat;

flesh and blood could stand it no longer. Whether they ignorantly supposed the cap.tain had control over the winds, or not, they murmured, and presently began to talk pretty high about making trouble on board. The captain got his pistols ready, probably to intimidate them; but it was not long before several boats from the laud, manned by persons who spoke a dialect unintelligible to any but Welchmen, came round the sloop, and finally the captain landed about one hundred and sixty, the other part choosing to remain on board, and go to Liverpool. 'As son as those were landed, it being about eleven o'clock, they washed themselves, and repaired to the rural church, to offer thanks undoubtedly for their safe deliverance. The others purchased some bread from the boats, and remained until the next morning, when they reached the wished-for port. Taking a seat on the stage, the writer arrived in London the next day in the evening.

Being returned to London after an absence of nearly ten months, before all thoughts of the stage were abandoned, Zerah went to Margate again; the prospect of promotion here was as small as formerly, and in a month he went back, concluding that this course was an idle and unprofitable speculation, and he began to think of other pursuits. He has not patience to record or even to think of his situation from September, 1820, to 1st of January, 1822. It is true he had bread to eat; it is true he was engaged in preparing some tragedy that might succeed in a theatre —five different pieces were written, but not one was either acted or printed. But the lack of occupation, the continual alienation of friends, who were becoming weary of contributing to his wants, and indeed the necessity of applying to individuals for their charity and benevolence, have left upon his mind a strong feeling of disgust, and it is painful to remember, much more to record, the history of such a period.

Were it not for the assurance he has that his father was actuated by a sincere but very misguided wish, by remaining in the midst of all his want and suffering to wait the anticipated approach of better days, his son would be disposed to look back upon his course with severe disapprobation. Still the first and chiefest portion of blame rests on those who being struck with the wonder, without suitable reflection proposed their plans; or being destitute of perseverance, suffered their plans to come to nought and left the ill-fated victim, who blindly put confidence in their.promises, to extricate himself from difficulty in the best manner that he could. And it is an inference left upon the author's mind, from the experience that he has had with Committees in England, that unless such associations have some common and abiding bond of interest to preserve their energies alive and united, the whole of them are worth less than one man with half a share of common courage and devotion to his work.

"About these days Zerah was sent by his father with some communication to Mr. Montagu. He does not recollect the nature of it, but it was evidently displeasing to his former friend. Mr. M. called on his servant to open the folding-doors at their fullest expansion, and in presence of some members of the family, formally ejected the boy from his tenement. Afterwards, however, he treated him with some civility and appearances of friendship. He was the author of a book called "An E ?say on the use of fermented liquors," in which he endeavored to call up the attention of his fellow-countrymen to the evils of Intemperance.

After lingering along in this unpleasant manner until October, 1821, Zerah had an opportunity of going into a school of respectable character at Highgate, near London, where he remained three months as an assistant. At the end of that term, he conceived the plan of starting a school for himself.

CHAPTER XI.

Education in England.—Zerah commences a day school.—The Bishop of St. David's.—Mr. Colburn's health begins to fail.—Dr. Young.—Decease of his father.—His return to America.— Receives two letters from the Earl of Bristol.

It was in the beginning of Januajy, 1822, that Zerah commenced the instruction of a small school, collected by his exertions, in such branches cf common English education as are usually taught in this country. It is with a peculiar satisfaction that he reverts to his commencing in this employment. Never before, unless when exhibited, had he any opportunity of feeling that he contributed aught to his own support. When sometimes he hears people wishing that they had his privilege of seeing the world, to think of the price at which he purchased this privilege, would suggest the idea that they little knew what it was which they desired.

To visit foreign lands may well be wished, both for the pleasure of contemplating human life in all its various forms, both rude and refined, as well as for the knowledge thus imparted beyond what books can communicate. But by him, thi3 pleasure has been purchased at so dear a rate, that he hardly knows if he ought to consider his course the best. One serious truth, however, he has learnt by his experience in life: that it is better for a man to depend on his own resources and exertions, than to make any calculation of being supported by the patronage of others. Let his calling be what it may, if honest, though mean and laborious, let him pursue it with all perseverance and industry—he shall be happier and better provided for, than while waiting upon the great, liberal in promises.

The number of scholars with which he commenced his school was quite insufficient to provide a full support for himself and his father, and on this account their accustomed applications to the liberality of others weTe not entirely discontinued.

As already stated, the opportunities enjoyed for the common instruction of children, are inferior in England to those in this country. Except a number of seminaries designed for teaching the higher branches of literatuie to the sons of the wealthy, and charity schools for the very poor, all the learning acquired by their children is obtained by attending at the numerous academies and schools that are started and carried on by private individuals. Of this class some are day-schools in the city, and others are boarding establishments in the adjacent suburbs and surrounding country. Some are superintended by men, others by women; and this being their only profession, they depend for their support on the qualifications they possess as instructers of youth.

As the law makes no provision for schools, it must necessarily follow, that every one being left to his own choice concerning the education of his children, some will be educated and others neglected; hence persons may be frequently met with, unable to read or write: hence the progress of general information among the people must be limited. A total ignorance of their own country, and its political relations to other countries, is perceptible in many, who seem alike destitute of those principles which, formed under the guidance of an enlightened mind, prepare them for sustaining properly their situation in moral and virtuous society; and on this account we need not be surprised by the frequent occurrence of crimes among them; we cannot much wonder, that youthful offenders, not over twelve and fourteen years of age, are sentenced to the House of Correction, especially when they have been trained to such courses by parents who value neither learning nor goodness.

The discipline of the common schools in England is different from ours. There is perhaps no teacher but feels' himself authorized to make use of the rod, when other measures fail of subduing or reforming the refractory or the indolent pupil. He is considered to possess a discretionary power, in the absence of the parent, to take that course which-his judgment may dictate as being best calculated to secure the obedience and improvement of the scholar; and therefore there is generally little complaint, so long as the subject of such government is not abused. That manual correction is always most salutary and efficient, we are far from supposing; but in reference to the scholars found in our country districts, it is perhaps a just re-

mark, that many parents seem so fond of their high notions of liberty, as even to wish their children may have unrestrained license to do as they please, lest the free spirit should be cramped, and the fine genius they think they discover in their sons be borne downand thwarted in its aspirations by the strictness of scholastic rules.

Time passed on with little variety in the teaching department for a few months. Mr. Colburn called at one time upon the Bishop of St. David's, who, ten years before, had become a subscriber for the book. He manifested a friendly disposition, and a prospectus was drawn up, stating the present situation and employment of the boy, and requesting all the benevolent to unite in raising a fund for his more permanent relief. This paper was signed by the Bishop, Sir James Mackintosh, Francis Place, and Basil Montagu, once more, and after all accomplished little, or nothing, as the other plans had done.

About the first of August, Zerah was dispatched on a subscription voyage to Edinburgh, Glasgow, and Belfast, with the above prospectus, but met with no encouragement. It was while in Edinburgh this last time, that Mr. Combe, the Phrenologist, sought an opportunity of taking the third cast of his face, and examined his head in order to discover some more light on that system. He returned to London, resumed his school, and continued in it until the sickness of his father compelled him to abandon it.

It was in December, 1822, that Mr. Colburn's health first began to decline; not indeed a victim to hard labor of body, but to something more destructive of health—labor and care of mind. It was now about twelve years since the commencement of his trials and anxieties in relation to his son. Should it be said that the first four years, up to the time of his visiting Paris, were years of prosperity,—which would not be true, in view of the Boston business and the trouble subsequently incurred on that account—for the last eight years, he had been continually harassed and perplexed; his feelings had often been highly excited by favorable offers

made, and while too much depending on them, he was little prepared for the shock of disappointment which heavily and suddenly came. At different periods of the time, he had been prevented by poverty from procuring comfortable food, and at length his constitution, once strong and robust, besian to sink.

The Earl of Bristol had now returned from his foreign tour; Mr. Colburn wrote to his lordship, but received an answer in which the Earl excused himself from any present interference in his affairs. In this situation matters lingered along until the summer of 1823, when the Bishop of St. David's introduced the writer to the notice of Thomas Young, M. D. and Secretary to the Board of Longitude. This gentleman had conceived the idea of making the talent of the young man profitable to himself, if not to the community. Accordingly after receiving such occasional instruction as the Doctor was able to give, on account of his numerous medical and scientific avocations, on the eighteenth of January, 1824, he received his first payment for calculations made by him in ascertaining the places and variations of certain stars. This new employment, evidently'more suitable to his natural turn of mind than any thing in which he had been engaged for several years, seemed also to promise a better support than they had long obtained. On account of the rapid decline of his father's health, it had become necessary for him to close his school, and it was hoped that as their circumstances seemed to brighten up in their aspect, he might recover, and yet live to return to his family.

Notwithstanding the tone of discouragement which his physicians held, he had never given up the idea of recovery and returning to his family. In view of the encouraging prospects connected with the employment furnished by Dr. Young, he expressed his opinion that in a year and a half he should have his preparations made to revisit his long deserted home. Towards the close of his life, Dr. Young commenced visiting him, but the lack of necessary comforts heretofore, and it may be want of suitable medical treatment, had so far contributed to the strength of his disorder, that by a gradual and sure progress of consumption, he wasted away until February 14th, when he breathed his last. At the time of his decease, his age was 54 years, 3 months, and 8 days.

As it was alone for the sake of his son that he left his home and country, and through the strength of parental affection, felt an obligation to remain with him, and exercise a watchful care and oversight for his interests, it may be proper for his son to remark, that though he has long been convinced a better way might have been selected, still he is bound to retain a grateful sense of his father's zeal and perseverance in his behalf. He considers the sentiment perfectly correct which was expressed in a letter received some time after from James Dunlop, Esq. "I have no hesitation in saying that he must have had many excellent qualities to inspire his son with such strong feelings of devotedness as to induce him to remain with him through every form of suffering, notwithstanding the brilliant prospects presented to his view."

He was a man that feared nothing in the discharge of what seemed to be duty; habitually plain in speech and manners. While at home with his family, he was attentive to their wants, on some occasions working one, two or three nights in succession to provide for them in a newly settled country; and when absent engaged to devise means for an honorable return, that he might make unto them full reparation for the trials incurred during their long separation. Two days before his end, when conversing on the probability of his decease, he told his son it was best that he should return to his mother as soon as he could make the necessary arrangements. The time had not unfrequently been, when by leaving his father, Zerah might have availed himself of the patronage of others. This however was a step perfectly obnoxious to his feelings. No doubt it would have been better for himself as to pecuniary advantage, but the recollection of such a course would not have been more agreeable than that which now fills his mind.

In the evening after his death Zerah called at the house of Mr. Montagu to communicate the intelligence. A little sympathy was expressed; during the. moments that he staid, he saw the Rev. Edward Irving, who was then commencing his race of eccentric popularity. He was a man of large frame, a cranium and countenance indicative of a strong mind. He did not hear him speak, but his character is doubtless well known from his writings.

From Mr. Montagu's he went to Mr. Dunlop's house. This gentleman had long been his friend. Liberal in good advice, as well as in pecuniary assistance, he had formerly tried to dissuade him from an Actor's life. When he abandoned that undertaking, he still continued ready to assist. Advancing some money for immediate exigencies, he recomYnended him to wait on Lord Bristol, and make known the change in his situation. We have already said, that on a former application, his "lordship saw fit to refuse entering into Mr. Colburn's concerns again. Notwithstanding, at a subsequent time, he made a liberal donation, on seeing the paper patronized by the Bishop of St. David's, in June, 1823. From that time Mr. C. had no communication with him.

The day after his father's death, Zerah took the stage and went down to Brighton, where his lordship then was. The earl received him kindly, and without casting the least reflection upon the deceased, gave him directly to understand, that his friendship for the son still remained. He said that if the object of his former patronage was not so old, (now in his twentieth year) he would still be at the expense of educating him, even through Cambridge University. But on learning the wish of Zerah to return to this country immediately, he said he would contribute with others to this object. With this encouragement, Zerah returned to London to jnake the necessary preparations for the funeral.

In that city, the custom on such occasions differs a good deal from that of America. The corpse is seldom interred until the fifth day, and more frequently it is a week or more between the de-

cease and inhumation of a person. Before interment, the corpse must be seen by persons appointed for the purpose of ascertaining if the death was natural, or caused by unfair means: two aged females came in to see the corpse on the present occasion. On the eighthday, 82d February, the body was removed to the mansions of the dead, followed by his son, John Dunn Hunter, and two other acquaintances.

John Dunn Hunter was a man of brief but interesting notoriety. As his "Narrative," published in London, has not probably been in the hands of every one who may read this book, it may be proper to say that he was from America: of his parentage and ir-' fancy he knew nothing; his first dawning perceptions were developed among a tribe of Indians in the Arkansas territory. Whether he was the offspring of white parents who had been murdered, leaving him to the mercies of the sons of the forest, or whether born an Indian, he could not himself decide. He was retained among them, and instructed in the science of their warfare, until several years had passed away.

At length his tribe formed a plan for surprising a defenceless company of another tribe, and exterminating them at once. Hunter conceived the bold design of giving the exposed party timely warning of the meditated attack. The conflict in his soul, between savage honor, in remaining true to his own party, and sympathy for the objects of their hatred, was severe, but well sustained. He knew that to give the necessary information would expose him to the fearful vengeance of his tribe; therefore he resolved to abandon them forever, and seek the white man's home. His attempt was successful,—the threatened company escaped, and Hunter made his rapid way unmolested, to the white settlements. The singularity of his case excited attention, he was put to school, and became gradually civilized. He adopted the name of John Dunn, from one of his patrons, and that of Hunter, on account of his Indian pastime and delight. In 1823 he visited England. He was a man of high principles and a noble spirit—a fine specimen of what, if not Indian primogeniture, yet at least, the influence of Indian greatness and education, could do to raise the mind to its native grandeur and elevation, and afterwards of the reforming power of civilized and moral society.

Notwithstanding his opportunities for observing the advantages conferred by civilization, and, as its source, the Gospel, Hunter stated that there was a mystery in the Christian religion which his mind had never been able to reconcile and embrace. This fact 'may be adduced as showing the strong power of earlyimpressions, when even the light of civilization could not dispel the darkness brooding on his mind, or overcome the notions he had imbibed of the Great Spirit, from the traditions and superstitions of his early associates. He returned to America about the time that Zerah Colburn did, sought his way to his former friends, and was killed by a treacherous Indian near Texas, in 1828.

The interval between the burial of his father, and his departure for America, was occupied by Zerah in making astronomical calculations for Dr. Young. He was able to earn about nine dollars (two pounds) per week at this business; it is likely that if he had continued in this employment, he would have become more ready and perfect by practice, so that he might have doubled this sum, and been in a way to lay up money even in so expensive a place as London. Some of his friends circulated a subscription paper for raising money to pay his passage home, and about thirty eight pounds were thus obtained. Lord Bristol had already put down his name for ten pounds: on the fourteenth of May, Zerah called upon the Earl to take his final leave. The interview was such as to leave on his mind a still higher opinion of his noble patron. His lordship inquired how much money had been subscribed; on learning the amount, he said, "If you have need of twenty-five pounds more, you shall have it." Zerah was not prepared to ask any more, but the Earl left the room a moment, and returned with a check on his banker to that amount. He then said, "If on your arrival

in your country, you still find yourself in a situation to need as much more, you may draw upon me for it." Expressing the kindest interest in his future welfare, he strongly urged him to peruse attentively the books he had formerly given him, saying, "Remember your best friend tells you to do it;" and requesting his young friend to write to him as soon as he reached his home, he bade him farewell.

Out of the above sum, j£63, after making a few necessary purchases for a voyage at sea, all but £25 was paid to different persons in low circumstances, with whom his father had unsettled accounts. This appropriation of money was never contemplated by those who had subscribed to give Zerah a passage home, but it was a gratification to his own feelings. And then came the hour of parting, with all its pleasures and its pains. There is something touching in the idea of tearing up all the social connections of twelve years of youth, and leaving the scene of the sweetest as well as of the bitterest recollections—alone—without companion or guide, to turn the back upon one world, and over the wild waste of waters to seek another home. On the way to the land of his birth, he felt as a stranger. He left England with a high regard for the people among whom he had passed the most interesting season of his life, though he had long desired to return to America: although his opinion of the superiority of our free institutions was high, (and that opinion has been confirmed by nine years' residence here,) still he remembers the land he has left with kindness, and can say with the Poet,

"England, with all thy faults I love thee still."

It was on Monday, May 17th, that, rising before the sun, he was on his way to take the stage for Liverpool, where he arrived the next day. He had letters from James G. King (son of the late Rufus King) to Mr. Archibald Gracie, an American merchant residing in that city, by whose exertions and influence about 36 dollars were collected and handed over to him. This was a very seasonable supply, as without it, he would have

been nearly pennyless on his arrival at New York. After being detained a week, he embarked on Tuesday, May 25th, for his native land.

As the talent possessed by Zerah Colburn had always been different from that of other people,. so had been his situation in the world. Hence it need not be strange if his views and feelings were peculiar in embarking for America. He had a mother, four brothers and two sisters, but he had not seen them for thirteen years; he knew not their circumstances —how well or how poorly they were enabled to provide for themselves; when he left them he had a father, though virtually lostto them. Now that parent was gone, and it was left his painful task to tell the widow and the orphan how he died. In Europe, after all his disappointments and sufferings, he was just learning how to support himself; now in a country of different habits and customs he was to-strike out a new course of action.

All these were circumstances calculated to embarrass his mind: but on the other hand, he was going to the home of his childhood, to resume the long alienated relations of the domestic circle. He was going to America, the land of freedom, of equal rights—the land, if any there be beneath the sun, where each individual may see the path of industry, virtue, honor, and comfort, thrown out before him in common with his neighbor;—the land which his imagination had pictured out, with all its variety of fertile mountains, plains and vallies, as approaching nearer to the dreams of fancy than all the world besides.

One feature peculiarly interesting to him was the republican simplicity and equality of manners which he expected universally to find. Wearied and disgusted by the pomp and state surrounding many who had little besides wealth or title to recommend them, he hoped to see that merit alone gave eminence among his fellow citizens. In many instances he has been disappointed—he has found much of wouldbe greatness among them—the affectation for something for which as yet neither nature nor superior virtues or qualifications has endowed them. Still may our system remain—still may the children of the fathers of our liberties use their best exertions to preserve the sacred trust committed to them at so dear a price of toil, and peril, and blood. May our patriots and statesmen feel that the information, the integrity and virtues of the great community, will most effectually perpetuate our country's weal—let them labor for the extension of these, and we may hope that as population increases, our nation shall increase in durability. and strength.

The vessel in which he sailed, brought over three other passengers; two were Englishmen, and one a Virginian, a young man who had visited England for the purposes of education and travel. How well he had profited by his opportunities, might appear from his profane and obscene conversation, his drinking and fighting. Being occasionally cheeked by the writer for his improprieties, he, because he could think of no more opprobrious epithet, would retort by calling him "the Methodist Preacher," a name which the subject of it considered as disgraceful as the young man who insultingly used it. He had at that time not the most distant idea that in less than eighteen months, he should look upon that calling and denomination as the happiest, most useful, and honorable in the world. In addition to his other acquirements, the young man seemed to possess a very acute discrimination between the privileges of " gentleman," and " plebian;" showing very clearly, that however he might enjoy himself as lord of the blacks, he would feel circumscribed in his feelings and movements among republican New Englanders.

After a passage of thirty days, during which they experienced the usual varieties of fair and foul weather, storm and calm, heat and cold, the ship Euphrates was safely moored at the wharf in New York, and American soil was speedily pressed, if not kissed, by the glad traveller, having been absent from 1 ft twelve years and three months. Of this time, eighteen months were spent in Paris, nine years in London, and the remainder in travelling in England, Ireland, and Scotland.

Being safely landed in this city, he delivered such letters of introduction as he had brought from London. Joseph Grinnell, a benevolent member of the society of Friends, took considerable interest in his situation, and introduced him to Professor John Griscom. They expressed a desire to provide a suitable employment, that might induce him to settle in NewYork, and spake of a situation in the High School, which they were hoping soon to see in operation. These friendly efforts were very gratifying to Zerah, and he then thought it probable that after visiting his friends in Cabot, he should return and place himself under their patronage.

Accordingly after staying five days in New-York, he took passage in the steamboat for Albany, proceeded thence to Whitehall, and there hired a man to carry him on to Cabot, and arrived at his mother's house, Saturday, July 3, about sunset. Not knowing who lived there, they inquired of an elderly woman who was at the door, if she knew where the widow Colburn lived 1 She replied that she was the woman. On hearing this, the stranger got out of the waggon and made himself known as well as he could. Many have inquired if his relations knew him. Even his own mother was as ignorant of the child she had nursed and provided for until he was six years old, as if she had never seen him before. Hence he is inclined to discredit what many have advanced about the power of secret, mighty instinct, drawing separated friends to each other. However, he contrived to make himself known, and his brothers and sisters were willing to admit his claims to kindred. He too needed information; he could not distinguish or remember one of his family. The place was different from his expectations, as his mother had dis posed of her former residence, and their situation in life was much worse than he had hoped to find it.

Mrs. Colburn was left in very difficult circumstances by the departure of her husband. She had at that time six sons and two daughters, the oldest of her children being only fourteen years old. She was a remarkable woman, and that probably her companion knew, or it would seem he never could have consented to leave her with such a heavy responsibility on her hands. The money which he left in her care when he was with his family at Norwich, Vermont, in April, 1811, was applied to the liquidation of debts in which the farm was involved, and except this, he made no calculation or provision for his family for twelve years. During this time, his boys were growing up, evidently needing a father's influence and example to go before them in their youthful path, but they had it not. Mrs. Colburn managed as well as she could, made such arrangements as seemed most advantageous, and incessantly toiled with her hands in the house and in the field, in order to preserve the little farm. At length she bargained it away for one more commodiously situated for her present state, and by a course of persevering industry, hard fare, and trials such as few women are accustomed to, has hitherto succeeded in supporting herself, besides doing a good deal for her children. She is now in her 65th year.

When Zerah arrived at home, and found what her situation was, though unable to relieve her from her burdens, he soon abandoned the idea of going back to New-York, three hundred miles away from his relations, to seek a permanent settlement, and wrote to that effect to his friend Joseph Grinnell. It is possible that he would have found it to his benefit to have returned; but home was very agreeable, and besides he had so long bee immured in a large city that he felt very unwilling to forsake a place that appeared so delightful as his native hills, for the confinement of a town life. As he had been requested, he wrote on the 6th of July to the Earl of Bristol, stating his arrival, his circumstances, &c. He discovered before long that he was not in a situation to be of any essential service to his family, and that it was becoming important that no more time should be lost. He commenced a school in Cabot, which he taught two months. In October he received the following letter from the Earl of Bristol.

"*London, Jlug.* 6, 1814. "Lord Bristol received with pleasure Mr. Colburn's letter with the account of his safe arrival in America. If he should want any pecuniary assistance in September, he may write without reserve to apply for it; and Lord Bristol will be disposed to grant it; but it must be only a small sum, as Lord Bristol has so many claims upon him. Lord Bristol learns with great satisfaction that Mr. Colburn has read the books he gave him with so much attention. He strongly recommends to him to read Butler's Analogy again, and again. Mr. Colburn will like it better and better every time he reads it. His excellent understanding will not fail to find in it those sound and large views which will lead him to satisfactory results upon all the main points of morals and religion.

"Lord Bristol offers to Mr. Colburn his sincere and cordial good wishes."

The receipt of this letter was very agreeable. Zerah wrote in reply that he should be glad to receive some further assistance, and after closing his little school, waited a few days in thinking what course he should next adopt. Having received an invitation to act as an assistant in an Academy in Fairfield, State of NewYork, connected with Hamilton College, he went to that place in December; but finding his prospects there quite different from what he had anticipated, he made arrangements for returning to Burlington, Vermont. A few days before he left he received the following letter from the Earl of Bristol. *"Nov.* 28, 1824. "I have received your letter of the 21 st October, and rejoice to hear you have such good prospects. You may draw upon me for £25 sterling, payable at Messrs. Coutts', Strand, London, bankers, and your draft shall be duly honored. With regard to the other part of your letter, I have only to request you to read over attentively a second time, Butler's Analogy and Paley's Evidences, and I shall be glad to hear from you, with such observations as occur to you in reading those excellent works. I think so highly of your understanding, and of your disposition, that it will be a

real pleasure to me to direct your mind in those most important studies; and finally to see you arrive at those results which will secure you equally against the dangers of skepticism on the one hand, and of a fanciful religion on the other. Butler's Analogy should be read over and over again, till you have made his thoughts your own. I should advise also a repeated revision of Paley's three works —his Natural Theology, his Evidences, and his Horse Paulina?—which last is a work inferior to none. When your understanding has laid a broad and sure foundation, books of practical piety and devotion should then. be habitually read; and Doddridge's Rise and Progress of Religion in the Soiil, is of itself a library; and he who has fully imbibed it, and daily practises its contents, will have nothing left to wish for. We must always remember that it has pleased Providence to form us of *heads* as well as *hearts,* and that both must be brought into his service. I knew you when you was quite a child, and always thought you destined to be a source of comfort to your family and of usefulness to your neighborhood.—I hope from my heart that God will of his infinite goodness direct and bless you in all you undertake; and that he will make you a happy man and a good Christian. I am, with real regard,
Your sincere friend and humble servant, Bristol."

By the same mail he received a letter from James Dunlop, Esq. with directions for him to draw upon Robert Dickson, of New York, for ten pounds. This was an unexpected donation, but very acceptable, as he was on trie point of starting for Burlington, and had little cash on hand.

The above letters are inserted, not because the writer is conscious of meriting the encomiums of his noble friend, but to furnish the reader with a more full idea of his lordship, than perhaps could be gathered from the preceding pages. They are the last communication that he has received from the Earl. He wrote to his lordship on receiving the last, and twice since, but from some cause has received no reply. Did the Earl receive

his letters, doubtless he had good reasons for the course he took, though it seems probable that some accident has attended the transmission of them. Let the cause of the Earl's silence be what it may, the remembrance of his kindness will ever be grateful to the honored object of it, and with many other obligations received will incite him as far as he is able, if not to repay, yet at least to show that he is not undeserving of the efforts of his friends.

CHAPTER XII.

Zerah removes to Burlington, Vermont. —His religious experience. —Joins the Congregational church.—Becomes dissatisfied with their doctrines, and unites with the Methodist Society.—Begins to hold religious meetings.

It was about the middle of March, 1825, that leaving Fairfield, Zerah Colburn removed to Burlington. Here he commenced the instruction of a number of young ladies and gentlemen in the French language, with a view to his present support, while he resumed his classical studies, thinking it possible that if every thing went on according to his wishes, he might eventually receive a Diploma from that Institution when duly qualified. In April he received a return from his draft on the Earl of Bristol; as he was in a situation that promised all that he needed then, and his future prospect was not bad, he considered it would be no wrong done to the liberality of the Earl, while it would be a small and just compensation to his Mother, for her trials on his account, to place this sum at her disposal. He accordingly gave her between eighty and ninety dollars, and continued in his studies and his French class until the summer.

The writer is disposed, when he takes a retrospect of the past scenes of his life, to think with pleasure upon the numerous expressions of kindness received from individuals of every country, name, party, or religious sect, with whom he has come in contact. Probably no other person before was ever so successful in the race of popularity; and as heretofore, it would be still his delight, were he able, to pursue a course that would perpetuate those friendly feelings towards him. It is with regret that he expresses his fear of the possibility of his doing this. Formerly, when his only peculiarity was an uncommon endowment of mind, all could contemplate and applaud without jealousy or distrust; but now, at a riper age, when led to realize the importance of acting not only for this world, but also for one which is to come; of seeking, not merely the favorable notice of man, but also the honor that comes from God, he feels unwarranted to expect a kinder reception from all classes than has fallen to the lot of other, greater, and better men. Nevertheless, in his religious, or rather his ministerial capacity, he deems it probable that the memory of his former distinction has sometimes procured a favorable reception, which would have been reasonably denied to his other talents, and while flattered, he wishes to be thankful too.

From an early age Zerah had been accustomed to meditate on the subject of religion. Though he had never received any particular, instruction, except an occasional remark from his father, yet he can look back to a very early period of his life, when his mind, though puerile and dark in its ideas, was raised to consider that glorious Being, whom the Christian worships as his God and Saviour. The New Testament was among the first books given to him by different friends, and he was accustomed to read its contents with satisfaction; as a natural consequence he became disposed to embrace its tenets as true, long before he had any idea of the different interpretations that are given for or against it by the friends or enemies of revealed truth.

At the period alluded to, however, his situation was unfavorable for any direct and permanent benefit to be received. Moving round with rapidity from place to place for the purpose of exhibition, continually coming in contact with an endless variety of characters and scenes, he had little opportunity for sober reflection. Many indeed who called to see him being of a serious .ve him religious books and tracts, which he always read with interest, and perhaps by the bless-

ing of God, such things had a happy tendency in preserving his mind from an infidel bias. He does not recollect that he ever had any desire or inducement to reject a belief in the existence of God, the truth of the Scriptures, or the eternity of the separate conditions of the righteous and the wicked.

It has already been observed, that while at Westminster school, his teachers required a weekly lesson in the Catechism of the Church of England. He was one day in the shop of Francis Place, who from a poor journeyman tailor had risen to extensive business, but who was a follower of Thomas Paine. Some of the men employed there made an attempt to lead him to ridicule the doctrine contained in the second commandment, but the attempt excited his disgust and horror. Still he was generally negligent, though occasionally thoughtful. His views of vital godliness were principally confined to outward reformation, and morality of deportment, connected with a form of devotional exercises. Of experimental piety, he had, for years, no more consistent idea than he had of the inhabitants of a fairy land. It is true he had learned that the Methodist denomination held to a certain spiritual witness, or divine communication to the believer, which rendered him happy; but ignorant as he was of the «ense of Scripture, he concluded that it was merely by producing an excitement of the passions that they attained to this experience, and in hie heart he despised and pitied them for their ignorance. He occasionally visited the houses of worship of the Established Church, but their sermons were either unseasonable or without reference to the grand point of the sinner's case and the Christian's hope, so that he derived no benefit from them.

When his father died, the first and most effectual conviction he had ever felt, was impressed on hia mind of the pressing importance of being in a state ©f preparation for a similar event. During the succeeding three months that he remained in London, his feelings were a good deaHnterested in the subject, but he had not been able to come to any sat-

isfactory conclusion previous to his arrival an Cabot. After he reached his native town, he became acquainted with a number of families, both among the Methodist and Calyinist people, and he found that whatever might be their differences on other points of doctrine, they held the same testimony in relation to Christian experience; and at length he began to think he had previously been in an error.

Now he was assailed by good, affectionate advice and exhortations to seek the salvation of God. He evaded these kind attacks, by promising himself that in four years he would commence in earnest in this important work. In this he manifested an erroneous view of religion; thinking that a proper attention to it would interfere with the honorable avocations of life, he designed to put it off until the period when he should probably be settled in the world. He had occasional discussions with the resident Calvinistic minister of the town, but some points which the clergyman tried to support were very new to him, and it. is doubtful if he was ever benefited by these discussions. It is his opinion that the course pursued by the gentleman alluded to, was little calculated to, direct and inform his inexperienced mind, but the subject appeared to him of such importance, that he was frequently engaged in examining it.

One morning he went into his schoolhouse some time before the hour for the scholars to collect; he sat down, and began to revolve the subject in his mind. Something suggested to him the following train of thought. "Supposing that there was one way alone by which I could live wholly according to my inclinations, in all the vain and unholy desires of unregenerate nature; suppose that this way was to dethrone the Father of Mercies, plant my foot on his neck, and consign Him to everlasting shame and sorrow, and I had power sufficient, would I do it in order to enjoy my own desires 1" It will not surprise the serious reader to be told that, conscious of inherent rebellion »f heart, he trembled and durst not acknowledge to himself what indeed was the correct answer to this inquiry.

Another proof of his ignorance in spiritual things, appears from a little conversation he heard, between a pious female, and a man who has since died in faith, but was at that time unconverted. In her remarks she observed that he had been striven with by the Spirit of God. Zerah was very much struck on hearing any thing like this. What, thought he, is it possible / Is there any 6uch case as the Eternal Spirit striving with man / However, he forbore from asking any explanation of the subject.

While in Fairfield, N. Y. his attention was a good deal fixed on the subject, and on one occasion he called upon the minister who was then preaching to the Presbyterian church, for advice, but the communication he received was not of any great benefit, and he made no sensible advances in the way to God. One reason, perhaps, was, he had not yet come to a fixed determination to seek until he should find what there was to be enjoyed in the Christian's privilege. It was not until after he had removed to Burlington, where he considered himself permanently settled, for months if not for years, that he seriously set out in the great undertaking. Having much leisure time, and a retired situation, except during the hours devoted to his French classes, he thought within himself; "I have put off the period of seeking and serving the Lord until four years shall have elapsed. Before that time comes, I may be dead and my destiny sealed forever." He durst neglect no longer; without counsel, encouragement, or exhortations from any living creature, having only his Bible and his closet, he commenced by much prayer and frequent perusal of the Scriptures to seek the salvation of God. If any poor, benighted soul might ever say he knew not the way to approach the mercy seat, he might. All his confidence was built upon a sentiment he then embraced as cordially as he advocates it now, namely that God was willing to be approached by the prayer of the sincere and the humble; that what he knew not the Almighty would teach him, if he asked with earnestness and perseveran-ce.

Soon after he commenced in this course, he procured "The Rise and Progress of Religion in the Soul," by Dr. Doddridge, a book which was of much assistance to him in obtaining correct views of himself and his God. He was thus engaged, during five or six weeks; as he proceeded, the exercises of his mind, which were at first very superficial as to depth of pungent feeling, became more distressing and sorrowful, until he feared that his day of acceptance was passed forever. Resolved, however, to know the worst of his case, he persevered in the pursuit, and at length obtained such a change in his views, while engaged in secret prayer, pleading the promises of God, that he considered it needless for him to make any further efforts until he had consulted the clergyman, and ascertained what he must next do to obtain the favor of God.

Accordingly he called on Mr. Preston, and obtaining an interview, entered very fully into a statement of his feelings and exercises. After hearing him through, and putting a number of questions to him, Mr. Preston told him, that if bis account was a correct one, he might believe that he had experienced religion. This was news indeed; he knew that in some respects, his views had been greatly altered, but was not prepared to imagine that without a more striking experience, he had come into the glorious liberty of the people of God. When repairing to the house of the clergyman, he ae much expected to be told that he was endowed with angelic powers, as that he was a child of grace. Still, he concluded that his spiritual guide knew better than he did; that he would not mislead him, and therefore for the present, his mind was at rest.

It may appear strange to some, that Zerah should now and on a former occasion, go to others with his feelings, in order to receive instruction, because the course is so different from the diffidence which awakened sinners commonly feel. The true reason was this; he does not recollect that the time ever was when he should have been afraid or ashamed to own that he needed the mercy of God; and it so happened, under existing circumstances, that he must have adopted this measure, or else have remained destitute of the instruction that he required.

While he was in Fairfield, his mind was engaged in the proper selection of a calling for the business of his life. It then appeared to him, that the duties of a minister of the Gospel were the most honorable, useful, and pleasant employment that a man could select, if he were faithful to his work, and he resolved in his own mind, if he should experience religion, that he would devote himself to this sacred office. Now his former resolution immediately recurred to his mind, and without reserve he made his intentions known to his friends.

A few days after this visit to. Mr. P. , it was proposed to him to unite with the church; he procured a copy of the church creed and covenant. He feels no disposition to insinuate that any thing dishonorable or like duplicity, was resorted to, to induce him to subscribe to the articles of faith, held by the Congregational church in Burlington. He was not flattered nor urged to embrace their sentiments; but his difficulty arose from the want of those helps, which he afterwards obtained, to explain the 8th and 9th chapters of Paul's Epistle to the Romans, and some other Scriptures of similar import, in a manner that would not clash with the doctrines of free grace and moral agency. He always had a See ply seated aversion to the idea of unconditional election and reprobation, but now he was unable to deny that such sentiments were in the Bible, and therefore he subscribed to that creed, though he felt as though he should greatly rejoice in discovering some way to escape from this unpleasant captivity. No way as yet presented itself, and he made a public profession of faith in Jesus Christ, and united himself with the church in July.

The change produced in his feelings, was accompanied by a change in his present intentions as to a collegiate life. Heretofore he had been thinking of secular employment for a livelihood; and he therefore leoked forward with considerable resignation to the prospect of spending three or four years in college; but now having his mind established to preach the Gospel, he did not feel willing to devote so much precious time to the perusal of Latin and Greek authors, whose works would probably never be to him of any signal benefit in presenting truth to his fellow creatures for the salvation of their souls. What little experience he had obtained relative to such things. in England, was calculated to fill his mind with deep disgust, not against learning, but against such sermons as exhibit nothing of the preacher but his learning and skill, while his piety and the face of his Master «eem to be out of sight.

There are, it is true, some well meaning persons who ignorantly entertain a strong prejudice against great sermons. The preacher's work and subject surely are great, if any calling is, and he should labor to have his heart so enlarged with light and love divine, and his mind so well replenished and stored with the treasures of all useful science and knowledge, that he may always be able to show forth what the grace of God can make him; what he is himself anxious to be. In order to accomplish this, not only is a course of theological and other reading enjoined upon all licentiates m the Methodist ministry, but the propriety of the injunction visibly commends itself to every reflecting mind.

It would be singular in any who have only learning sufficient to perceive the value and necessity of more, to decry its importance. No man, perhaps, has a stronger desire to see his brethren in the ministry fully qualified in this respect than the writer. He is of opinion, that so far from being a hindrance to the usefulness of a minister of Christ, deep science and extensive learning, if properly employed, may be of great service. But, as it regarded his own course at the time, he abandoned the idea of obtaining a liberal education; he thought it would be the best and safest way, immediately to obey the divine conviction, calling him to this work, rather than absent himself from the field of labor, and

confine himself in a theological seminary three years, during which period of delay, he might die without having once performed the commission which he felt was entrusted to him. He would gladly have possessed the literary advantages resulting from years of study, but circumstanced as he' was, he did not feel himself authorized to consider them his first object of present pursuit.

Reflections of this nature determined Zerah to make preparations for entering immediately upon the duties of this work. It was not long before he ascertained that the ministers of the order with which he was now connected, were opposed to giving him a license at present to hold meetings in any clerical capacity. He was disappointed here, though he could not think he had any right to complain. They recommended to him to take up his residence in some school where he might acquire a further knowledge of divinity: not knowing but this was the best thing he could do, he returned to Cabot to reflect more at leisure upon its expediency and wait the openings of Providence.

It has already been stated, that he was not cordially satisfied with soma of the doctrines embraced by the f church in Burlington. A year before, he would have felt fully justified in rejecting them with scarcely a thought on their merits. Now, certain passages in Paul's Epistle to the Romans, on which formerly he had bestowed no attention, presented themselves to his mind; and instead of explaining them as he now would, to describe the design of the Almighty to confer temporal privileges of a civil and religious kind upon individuals named, not exclusively for their own sakes, but in allusion to their posterity, he concluded that they vindicated the creed of his brethren. In Cabot, his intimacy with Methodists and others, brought him in contact with some ideas on this point which had not previously occurred with so much force, and a more anxious spirit of investigation was excited. It was not long before the foundation of his doctrinal faith was a good deal shaken; but he did not dare rashly to receive the new sentiments that presented them-

selves. He had once moved too rapidly to a conclusion, and he was now cautioned to be deliberate and impartial; he revolved the subject long in his mind, with painful anxiety; for he felt that his happiness and usefulness in time, and very possibly his salvation in eternity, depended upon the choice he might make. He conversed freely with Christians of the different denominations; but he found his objections against the peculiar doctrines of the denomination with which he had been connected, to be rather increased. Were it necessary to the objects of this publication, he could state in detail a very distressing experience for months on this point. Suffice it to say, that the delays to which his mind was subjected now, might seem to be a just though severe reward for his former precipitancy. However he could not yet feel himself at liberty to join the Methodist denomination. The principal obstacles in his way were, the regard he had for the Congregational brethren as a people, and the fear of lying under the imputation of instability of mind; he was long undecidtd on this point, but at length concluded that it was solemnly incumbent on him as a Christian, and as one that looked forward to the office of a public teacher of divine truth, if he had subscribed to an error, to take the readiest and most public method of renouncing that error; he could never think that it would be right or even safe for him with his present view of the doctrines he had held, to remain in a situation from which the testimony would go forth to the world, that he was satisfied with them, and viewed them to be the essential truths of the immutable Jehovah. If others can, they may; he did not dare to do it; if he has ever felt any thing to be a duty, it is that he be decided in his belief, and to exert no influence directly or indirectly that may keep a part of his sentiments under any cover or disguise. He addressed a letter to Rev. Mr. Preston, the pastor of the church at Burlington when he joined, making known the change that had taken place in his mind, and requesting an honorable dismission and-recommendation. From some cause he received no reply; but having in his possession a certificate of church membership, which was handed to him when he left Burlington, it was judged that this would answer the purpose of a regular letter, and he was received into the Methodist Society in Cabot, in December, 1825.

The step which he thus took, without doubt, has caused many to wonder, who feel, perhaps, as he formerly did towards that denomination; he thinks he knows how to bear with them, and he sincerely hopes the time may come when they will be enlightened as he has been. Many have expressed a surprise that he should devote himself to the ministry of reconciliation, whereas by pursuing a proper course, he might, they say, have made himself rich and celebrated. In vindication of his course, he would observe, he has tried many countries, many varieties of life, many pursuits; lie has been smiled on by princes, and caressed by nobles and the great ones of the earth; his praise has been spread over continent, and island, and sea: but what are all these things *l* he feels that they are utterly insufficient to fill the living, restless desires of the spirit within, which being immaterial and immortal, can never find its hungerings and thirstings allayed by matter, or any thing of time and sense below. Perhaps he is justified in saying, that if these things could impart substantial joy, he should have been superlatively happy; from experience he knows that they cannot. But there is something that can;—not confined to sect or name, to rank or situation in life, but ready to be possessed and enjoyed by all who seek God in sincerity, and worship him in truth.

As to happiness, he feels that he has gained by the course he has pursued, and he is led to think that on the score of honor, he has not materially lost. Admitting that he had been educated for a scientific life; that he had risen to the most elevated station in the literary world, and had evinced a maturity of talent that would have commanded the admiration of all who had a mind sufficiently enlarged and cultivated to follow him in his deep and learned researches, still the witnesses of his merited fame would have been limited in number, because the generality of mankind might not have time or taste to investigate his claims to honorable distinction; but in his present calling, while he hopes that the profoundly learned may not scorn to approve the labors of the servant of Christ, he feels that if faithful to his work, his name shall live in the memory, the affections, and the prayers of his brethren; the church of God shall rejoice in hi3 fidelity and perseverance; and if some poor outcast from God, by his instrumentality, should be turned from the practice of sin to the knowledge, the service and enjoyment of religion, he is sure that pardoned soul will gladly remember the sound of his name. And more than all this, the honor that comes from God; the testimony of the most High, in approbation of bis work, must be taken into the account, if honor and fame are the great objects that deserve our chief pursuit and care.

It is because he believes the Scriptures, because he looks forward and expects a day will come when the faithful witness for Jesus shall be received to his heavenly home, with most cheering testimonials of his consistent and virtuous and useful career; because he expects the hour is approaching when honor shall be torn from those pursuits that falsely claim it here, and ascribed to its proper objects, that he feels satisfied with his lot and calling.

Notwithstanding his uniting himself with the Methodist Society, it was a long time before his mind was completely satisfied and at rest as to the unsoundness of the system he had abandoned; however he received permission to hold religious meetings, that he might try to talk and exhort a little for the improvement of his mind in such an exercise. The rapidity of his movements may be accounted for by remembering that it was now nearly a year since in view of the goodness of the work, he had fixed his eye upon it. He cannot speak of painful impressions leading him to this undertaking, such as many of his dear brethren in the ministry have had. It rather seemed that the Lord was disposed in the gentlest and most persuasive way to lead him along by holding up the fair and pleasing side of the picture to his view. He well knew how to catch the heart of his weak disciple; had he began by pointing out all the trials, and crosses, and sorrows of an itinerant preacher's life, it is more than probable he would have discouraged him from it in the beginning.

CHAPTER XIII.

Farther remarks upon his new calling.— Causes which led to this publication.— C onclusion.

Should any one who reads these pages inquire, what after all the varieties of his life, were the feelings with which Zerah engaged in this new employment, he would simply say that unacquainted with any reason why he might not dedicate himself to this work, he felt only its superlative importance, and felt that however fearful or unworthy he in common with others might be, the love of God, and the loveliness of his cause, incited him to go on.

The success of his first efforts in this new employment was doubtless discouraging to his elders in experience; indeed they were seldom called upon to approbate the labors of a young man so little qualified for acceptance or usefulness as the subject of this Memoir; and it is now a matter of surprise to him, that, discouraged and disgusted, they had not sent him home. But they bore with his weakness then, and for seven years they have held him up, trying to make him profitable to himself and others. During that period, he has been appointed to seven different circuits, in the eastern part of Vermont, excepting the first, which was Canaan in New Hampshire. As to his talents, acceptability, and usefulness, others are the proper judges. His attachment to the work, to the Methodist economy and doctrines, is as great as at any former time.

An allusion has been made to the probability, that now his character and intercourse with mankind will not obtain for him that very general approbation, which he received while exhibited as a boy of remarkable endowments in early life. Nevertheless, he feels that he has abundant cause of thankfulness that his way thus far has been prospered so much in this respect; and the kindness Of thousands to him personally, merits acknowledgmeut. How much of this may have been owing to the memory of his early gift, is not for him to say; but it has had its effect in rendering him more fully satisfied with the choice he has made.

He has been questioned a good deal in regard to his early talent, and the various circumstances connected with or growing out of its premature display, and not unfrequently has it been suggested to hhn to write a history of his life. Many circumstances have hitherto deterred him. The memory of the subscription business in London, has had its influence; a short time after the death of his father, at the instance of some of his friends he set about writing a brief sketch of his life, with a view to have it published. Mr. James Dunlop undertook to read it, and express his opinion relative to the propriety of its publication; but he thought it was not advisable to print it, on account of the manner in which the failure of different committees had been noticed in it: accordingly the project was given up. He brought the manuscript to this country, but by some means, that, and all the original papers from which it was prepared, have been lost, except a copy of the Boston Indenture, and this has been one reason for his unwillingness to commence writing.

The substance of what he could write would either be an account of his calculating powers, or a sketch of his situation for fourteen years of his life. Were it his opinion that a full account of his remarkable gift, and the methods by which he effected his calculations, would be of any service to the mathematical world, he should have published it long ago. He feels that he is warranted in saying that a case probably never occurred before, in which so much patronage was promised by the wealthy and great, that involved the subject of it in so much suffering and sorrow; but he

has doubted whether the knowledge of all this would add to the general information of mankind. Moreover the want of time to write, and then superintending the printing and sale of such a work, has been a hindrance.

At length his situation has become such that an effort was necessary to obtain some pecuniary means for supporting a wife and three little girls, over and above the contributions of the people among whom he has been laboring during the past year, and for want of any more promising employment, this has been undertaken. The most that he has supposed himself capable of doing by this publication, has been to present to the public a correct history of a very remarkable fact in the annals of the human mind, probably without a precedent; how far any of the facts here recorded, or of the Arithmetical rules at the end of the volume, may be beneficial to the reader, is not for him to say; but he hopes no injury will thence result to any one.,

In relation to the faculty of computation which he possessed, he would observe that in every particular, from its first developement to the present day, it has been to him a matter of astonishment. He has felt and still feels, that it was undoubtedly a gift from his Maker, and consequently designed to he productive of some valuable ends. What the specific object was is unknown. Was it to place the young man in a situation where he might be eminently useful in scientific labors If so, by neglect, or ignorance somewhere, that object remains frustrated. Was it that by rendering the young man so celebrated in early life, he might thus be introduced to the notice of the public when he came to address them on the great salvation 1 If the notoriety of his youth was designed as an introduction to him in his ministerial capacity, it would be a natural expectation that his talents as a Preacher would be equal, if not superior, to the striking displays-of his early precocity. This howevis far from being the case.

One good woman, when she heard of the case twenty-two years ago, formed an idea that he was thus endowed in or-

der to serve the interests of the church by bringing to light the mysterious periods alluded to in the prophecies of Scripture, and calculating when the great events therein foretold shall actually take place; but for this he feels himself as little qualified as any other person. Was it then designed for no greater object than a *lums naturce,* as if he had been born with two heads *1* He should feel unwilling to consider this the extent of the design of the Giver. What then was its intention? To those who believe the doctrines of Christianity and the illumination of one darkened mind a work more precious than any earthly interest, the case of 'Squire

B, mentioned at the commencement of the volume, might seem indicative of the real design of the faculty; for indeed it must be well pleasing to the Most High that all his various works lead men to a sincere acknowledgment of his true character; but this has been the only case of this description, that has occurred within his knowledge.

After all the reflection he has spent on this subject, he is constrained to consider its object as unknown, unless comprehended under the general one that the Almighty proposes to himself in all his works and gifts. Hence that both he, and all others who may know of his singular faculty, should hereby learn correct views of the great Creator, and from the record of his visible acts, be led to a suitable faith in Him, and proper feelings of devotion to His name.

Such as it is, this little book is now before the public. Its narrative has been almost entirely prepared from the author's recollection of the scenes he has passed through. He claims no merit on its account, except as the correct historian of events, many of which may be as void of interest to the reader, as their memory is unpleasant to the writer. He has not written all that he might have done in regard to the privations of himself and his father; nor in every particular been as minute concerning his situation in more prosperous days as some might have expected; he has endeavored to be as circumstantial in these respects as his judgment suggested » would be proper or interesting.

Concerning his situation during the last seven years that he has spent in the traveling connexion, it does not occur to him that many of the scenes that he has passed through would be worthy of any special notice in this lace, though the remembrance of them is very pleasing to him. He has found himself in an excellent situation to obtain a species of knowledge equally and perhaps more useful to himself than the little he had formerly gleaned from books,—the knowledge of men and things; and this is one thing which establishes in his mind the superiority of the traveling system above the plan of a settled ministry. He has met with a variety of treatment from the different characters among whom he has been laboring, but nothing has transpired to induce him to think of deserting his post, so long as he can possibly attend to its duties. As he has said in regard to his father, so he trusts that he feels no fear when in the discharge of what is evidently a duty;— here his safety lies.

Prom the darkness brought upon his own mind, while perplexed with the Calvinistic theory, and the effect upon his own enjoyments, he has ever esteemed it his duty to hold up the peculiar sentiments of Methodism, in such a conspicuous manner, that there might be no danger of confounding them with a different creed. This plainness of illustration, while it proceeded from the best motives, if he knew aught of his own heart, has sometimes been considered as the emanation of a contracted, proselyting spirit; perhaps when unconscious of any evil intention himself, his manner may not sufficiently have agreed with the apostolic caution "to avoid the very appearance of evil." It has ever been his study, in the dispensation of the word of the Lord, to avoid any ambiguity of expression, but to deal with his fellow men in such a manner, that when he shall meet them and his Judge together, they may not accuse him of keeping back a part of his faithful testimony.

While penning these lines, the thought presses upon his mind, that possibly before they ever come before the public, his labors on earth may be finished, and his race be ended. Should this be the case; should he speedily be destined to close his mortal concerns, consigning his family to the mercies of God, and his soul to the promise of his Redeemer, let him be permitted to remind such as may never hear the offer of salvation from his lips, of the obligation they are under to the Almighty; especially that while reading these pages, and reflecting upon the singular endowment of the boy, and the more singular varieties of his short but eventful career, they should feel that after all his opportunities, as some suppose, for enriching himself, the blessings of salvation appear to him the most durable riches, and the work of the preacher the most agreeable employment that he could pursue.

Were it in accordance with the general design of this book, exhortations might be subjoined to every class whose eyes may be placed upon what he has written; but he has little reason to think that written counsels would avail more than oral testimony. Such is the moral power of agency and of choice which man exerts, that in this present philosophising, skeptical age, each one will do as he pleases, for and against his God and his immortal interests. But an hour is coming when our principles will be tested, our works investigated, and the improvement made by us upon the gifts committed to our hands ascertained with awful and impartial scrutiny. May we all be prepared for that day. Amen.

A LIST OF QUESTIONS ANSWERED BY THE AUTHOR WHEN A CHILD.

In order to furnish those who never saw the writer while exhibited with a further opportunity to understand the nature of his gift, the following questions, answered by him, are inserted. They are not all, nor perhaps the most extraordinary ones that he has solved; but they are such as he can say were proposed to him. They are given as specimens of the character of the questions proposed to him, ajid the time employed in answering them. Other questions will be found interspersed through the Memoir, particularly on pp. 37, 38,39, from the London Prospectus.

In Boston, on his first visit, in the fall of 1810. The number of seconds in 2000 years was required. 730,000 days. 17,520,000 hours. 1,051,200,000 minutes. 63,072,000,000 seconds—Answer. Allowing that a clock strikes 156 times in 1 day, how many times will it strike in 2000 years *t* 113,880,000 times.

What is the product of 12,225 multiplied by 1,223? 14,951,175. What is the square of 1,449? 2,099,601. Supposing I have a corn field, in which are 7 acres, having 17 rows to each acre; 64 hills to each row; 8 ears on a hill, and 150 kernels on an ear; how many kernels on the corn field *1* 9,139,200.

In Portsmouth, New-Hampshire, June, 1811. Admitting the distance between Concord and Boston to be 65 miles, how many steps must I take in going this distance, allowing that I go three feet at a step? The answer, 114,400, was given in ten seconds.

How many days and hours since the Christian Era commenced, 1811 years *1* Answered in twenty seconds. 661,015 days. 15,864,360 hours.

How many seconds in eleven years *1* Answer in four seconds; 346,896,000.

What sum multiplied by itself will produce 998,001 *1* In less than four seconds, 999.

How many hours in 38 years, 2 months, and 7 days? Jn six seconds; 334,488.

At one time in London he was requested to square 888,888. He gave it correctly, 790,121,876,544; and afterwards multiplied this product by 49, making 38,715,971,950,656, being the square of 6,222,216.

OTHER CALCULATORS.

Since the author commenced writing this book, he has met with some gentlemen who saw him when quite a child, who have mentioned a circumstance, of which, if it ever existed, he has no recollection. It was in relation to his personal appearance, when engaged in studying out the answer to a question;— that his body immediately assumed certain contortions, as if he were affected with what is called St. Vitus's dance, which continued until he obtained the result. As he does not recollect that this circumstance has ever been mentioned to him by others, during the period in question, he is not prepared to give any account of the cause of such apparent nervous affection. That it was the case, he is not prepared to deny; he is not conscious of ever feeling such mental fatigue as should produce such corporeal distortion. Perhaps it might have been owing to nothing more than mere childish motions. He is at a loss to account for the silence of others in relation to this, if it actually proceeded from the nerves. He has also heard of another person who evinced an uncommon quickness in calculation, somewhere in the neighborhood of Troy, N. Y. who on a question being proposed was strangely seized with every symptom of the above named affection, and continued in a violent exercise until the answer was obtained.

The inquiry has frequently been made whether the writer ever became acquainted With any other persons who were endowed with a gift of mental calculation similar to himself. He thinks not, as to extent of solution. While he was exciting his share of public attention in London, the case of Jedediah Buxton was often introduced. This man had then been dead a number of years. A farmer by occupation, poor and unlearned, he displayed an extraordinary power of carrying on arithmetical processes in his head. The chief agent which enabled him to obtain results, was a gigantic memory; in Multiplication and Reduction perhaps it may be said that no problem was too large for his mighty effort. A sum proposed in the above rules, was retained in the mind, carried on, and answered correctly, to the astonishment of him who proposed it. That he was a long time engaged in studying out the answer will not appear surprising to the reader, when he is told that all his operations were accomplished by pursuing the common rules of arithmetic. The several processes of multiplying the multiplicand by each figure of the lower line, were preserved in their relative order and place as on paper, until the final product was found by the last addition. Where each line consisted of five, six, or seven figures, the mental effort must have been incredible. A question of this description would not perhaps be answered until the day after it was proposed.

It is recorded of him that having never witnessed a Theatrical performance, some of his friends took him to Drury Lane Theatre, to see Garrick in one of his principal characters; he was observed to sit motionless during the whole performance, and his friends concluded that he was absorbed in admiration of the scene. At the conclusion of the play, they asked him how he liked it. He replied, "such an actor went in and out so many times, and spoke so many words; another so many; the musicians in the orchestra performed so many times, &c. &c. giving a proof that if he was insensible to the fascination of the Drama, at least he could exercise his quick and powerful memory there as well as in any other place.

The Countess of Mansfield called upon Zerah Colburn, while he was first exhibited in London, and alluding to the singular gift he possessed, stated that she had a daughter, Lady Frederica Murray, who was about his age, and gave indications of superior skill in figures. He was afterwards invited to call at her ladyship's residence, and found the young lady did possess a certain degree of mental quickness uncommon in her sex and years. But her elevated rank, and the necessary attention to those pursuits which were more in accordance with her station in life, probably prevented her attending to that endowment. She was afterwards married to Colonel Stanhope, and dying young, her widowed husband, after the lapse of a few years terminated his existence by suicide.

The person who in the writer's judgment approached the nearest to an equality with him in mental arithmetic, was a youth from Devonshire county, in England, named George Bidder. This person did not begin to excite attention until after Zerah had retired from public exhibition in London, sometime in the year 1815. Bidder was at that time ten years old. Having never had any acquaintance with him, the author cannot speak correctly of the manner in which his talent was first communicated and exhibited., The only thing he ever hearfl on this point was, that his father being engaged in eome difficult sum, George answered it at once; that in view of his unexpected readiness, he was-put to school, and considerable pains were taken to train him for exhibition. This however may be as incorrect as some of the stories in circulation relative to the subject of this memoir. It is certain, however, that in London he never received that general patronage which his predecessor enjoyed.

Some time in 1818, Zerah was invited to a certain place, where he found a number of persons questioning the Devonshire boy. He displayed great strength and power of mind in the higher branches of arithmetic; he could answer some questions that the American would not like to undertake; but he was unable to extract the roots, and find the factors of numbers. The last time that the winter was in Edinburgh, he was informed that the lad was in study, under the patronage of a Scotch nobleman.

At different periods, Zerah Colburn has heard of a number of persons, whose uncommon aptness in figures rendered them subjects of astonishment to others. He thinks it is no vanity to consider himself first in the list in the order of time, and probably first in extent. of intellectual power. It would be very easy to indulge in speculations in regard to the increasing number of persons thus endowed; but speculation avails little in so exact a science as mathematics, and would profit nothing on the present occasion. It is his opinion that should a similar case occur again, and the talents and habits of the individual in other respects not be too discouraging, it would be a general benefit to the cause of learning to make his education a matter of public interest; that he should receive such discipline and cultivation of mind as the best instructors could furnish, and let the experiment be fairly tried. It then would be seen more clearly than in any other way what was the object of the gift, and if a valuable help is therein concealed, it would be made public, and thousands might share in its advantages.

The human mind is a machine of gigantic powers, and we may well conclude that not all, if indeed more than a few of its energies are developed. We look upon the continual accessions to the philosophical literature of the age; we admire the seeming increase of its latent faculties, when we compare the improvements that have been effected by the wisdom of modern days, with the imperfect glimpses of this radiant light that shone upon the darker ages, and we are ready to conclude that man is beginning to rejoice in the new creation; that faculties hitherto unknown, are for the first time imparted to our species. Would it not be a conclusion equally just, that the mind is not so different in its ability from what it ever has been, a.s the opportunities presented to bring that ability to light, and exhibit intellectual man in all the native powers bestowed by his Creator, now raised, refined, and regulated by suitable culture, and directed to those noble ends which shall more conspicuously show the great design of Heaven in placing within his scope such a mighty treasure?

Who is there but admires the success which has attended those philosophers, who being sceptical as to revealed religion, yet bent all their efforts to seek out new discoveries in natural science 1 Yet the moral darkness that covered their minds has imperceptibly spread its dreary influence upon their followers; but it should not be hence inferred that the lights of science destroy, by a legitimate influence, the force and power of moral truth; as well might it be supposed, that the beams of moonlight can eclipsethe lustre of the noon-day sun. Let the juster inference be, that as it is the sun which lends its brightness to the nocturnal planet, and renders it mild in aspect and salutary in its influence; so the true light of revelation can lend a beauty and impart a sanctified and holy power to any species of correct knowledge.

As in every other bounty of Heaven, so the blessings of a cultivated mind may be abused. Even they who deem "the wisdom that cometh from above," the only "durable riches," are in danger of being so struck with the fascinations of literature, as to lose themselves amid its flowery fields, not looking up to Ibe higher Source, whence emanates a light that shines not to dazzle or to lead astray. Still, knowledge is not in fault; but that devotedness which offers an unreserved sacrifice of *all* at its shrine. They who have never experienced the benefits of cultivation, may vainly adduce the barbarous sentiment, that "ignorance is the mother of devotion;" but a cursory glance at the present state of the world will abundantly show, that the happiness of mankind is the result of civilization in a great degree, but not solely. 16

And this is because religion has brought these treasures in her train.

Then let the subject be fairly understood; let those who prize learning, understand its true, though secondary importance, and let them pursue it in the various improvements it offers to the mind; and while penetrating more deeply into all its hidden mysteries, let them so employ the measure already attained, that even they who are disposed to think it incompatible with true, elevated piety, may perceive their error: thus the world shall be benefited, and the church incited with a greater ardor to lead her sons and her daughters to devote themselves to the search after deep, extensive and sanctified acquirements in this respect. If these views are correct, then it will of necessity follow, that the Christian minister, in common with his brethren, may and ought to render himself familiar with all learning that comes within his reach. Had the writer received such an education as he thinks he should have obtained, it is perhaps probable that he might not have given himself to the work of the ministry. It is possible that some other path of usefulness might have been pointed out, equally justifiable in his situation. But, had he been educated in the best

manner; had his youthful name been as distinguished for literary attainments, as it was for his extraordinary power of mind; and had he been called to spend his life in the sacred calling, the testimony of the former, and the more recent history of the church would show, that he was prepared by learning, only to be more extensively useful to his fellow creatures.

METHODS OF CALCULATION.

From the first discovery of Zerah's calculating powers, many persons endeavored to ascertain the processes of his mind in obtaining his answers. That he had a necessary process, was inferred from the motion of his lips, and other trifling circumstances, between the moments of proposing and answering the question. When he first commenced, he recollects of being taken up into the lap by different persons, who used every effort to lead him to a developement of his mode; conscious of his own inability, or not fully understanding the import of their inquiries, he would cry and be distressed. All this backwardness was not owing to ignorance of the methods he pursued; he rather thinks it was on account of a certain weakness of the mind, which prevented him from taking at once such a general and comprehensive view of the subject, as to reduce his ideas to a regular system in explanation.

As the faculties of his mind were gradually unfolded, he became more able to concentrate his thoughts on the subject, yet he does not recollect that he ever interested himself at all to investigate it, unless when questioned on the point by others. Two years passed away before he made any disclosure of his methods. The first that he made known was his rule for extracting the Square and Cube Roots. This, as well as the others, was disclosed without any premeditation on the subject; indeed every thing in regard to hie calculations was performed without any previous effort, except such as suggested itself on the spur of the occasion. He communicated his Rule of extracting Roots in t he following manner: He was invited to dine with Mr. Francis Baily, one of his first friends in London. After dinner, Mr.

Baily introduced some mathematical subjects, which he endeavored to explain to his young understanding. Suddenly Zerah said he thought he could tell how he extracted Roots. When he first began at six years old, he knew not the meaning of the common terms. Questions were proposed by asking what number multiplied by itself would make the given Square; what number multiplied twice by itself would produce the given Cube. The use of the term *Root* was explained to him while at Hanover by Professor Adams.

Rule.

In extracting the Square Root, his first object was to ascertain what number squared would give a sum ending with the two last figures of the given Square; and then what number squared will come nearest under the first figure in the given square when it consists of five places. If there are six figures in the proposed sum, the nearest square under the *two* first figures must be sought, which figures combined will give the answer required.

Suppose it be required to extract the square root of 92,416. First inquire what sum squared ends in 16? Ans. 04; here we have the two last figures of the Root. Next, as the sum contains five figures, inquire what number squared comes nearest to 9 *I* Ans. 3. Put them together, 304—the number sought.

If the square contain six figures, say 321,489, first seek what number squared ends in 89. Ans. 67; then what number squared comes nearest to 32*I* Ans. 5. Combine them,—567. If tlfe sum contain seven figures, the root nearest the *three* first figures must be taken; if eight, the root nearest under the/our first, and so on. The following is a Table showing the numbers that being squared, will give the several terminations which occur in squares.

It is thought that there is little difficulty, according %o the rule presented, in determining the two last figures of the root; it is obvious, however, that it requires a good share of quickness and discernment, in a large sum, to see which of the *four* roots in ordinary numbers or which of the *ten*, where 25 is

the termination *ii* the right one to be employed. Such discernment, however, the writer cannot impart. As he told a certain lady in Boston, who was urging him to tell her how he reckoned, so he may say now: "God put it into my head, and I cannot put it into yours."

The cube root is found by the application of the tame principle. Take for instance, 28,094,464. First, seek what number cubed, will end in 64. Ans. 04: then what number cubed, comes nearest under 28. Ans. 3. Combine them, 304, the root required. Should the given cube contain *nine* figures, the nearest cube under the *three* first places, must be sought. If the cube root of 182,284,263 be required, after finding the number that in its cube gives 63, namely, 67, seek the nearest cube under 182. 5 is 125: combine them, and you have 567.

From the annexed table it will be seen, that there is not the same latitude for mistaking in the root of a cube number, that there is in extracting the square root. Some difficulty, however, exists; for instance, if the given cube end in 08, it will be a question whether 02 or 52 will be correct; and so of all similar cases.

Table for the Cube Root. gCp-Probably the reader has already perceived, that these Tables can apply only to numbers that are exact squat eg and cuius. KULE FOR FINDING THE FACTORS OF NUMBERS.

It has been the general sentiment of the mathematicians of Europe, that no rule existed for discovering the factors, or component integral parts of a given whole. To ascertain them, was an operation performed by Zerah Colburn from the commencement of his career. It was an operation attended with more difficulty than any other that he performed. / The manner of proposing questions of this nature was, "What two numbers multiplied together will produce such a given number?" Much interest to learn his method prevailed, but for upwards of three years he was unable to disclose it. It was on the night of December 17, 1813, while in the city of Edinburgh, that he waked up, and speaking to his father, said, "I can tell you how I find

out the factors." Hie father rose, obtained a light, and beginning to write, took down a brief sketch, from which the rule wag described, and the following tables formed.

Rule.

Supposing the factors of 1401 are required; refer to the table headed 01; 01 is of course a commoi factor to all numbers: take 03; as 67 multiplied by 3 gives 01, increase it by prefixing hundreds, and multiplying, thus: 3x167 =501; 3x267=801; 3x 367=1101; 3x467 =1401. Now if 467 be a prima number, these two tire all the factors that will produce 1401. Consult the table for 67—will 3 X 89 make 467? No. Will 3x189? No. 7x81 exceeds it; 9 will not divide a number which is not divisible by 3. 11 x 97 exceeds it: so will 13x59. It will be found that 467 is a prime number; therefore 3x467 are the only two factors of 14,201.

Take another number,—17,563; 03x21, with the ontinual prefix of hundreds and thousands will bring you to 5821 x3=17,463; the addition of another hundred will increase it too much. 07x09=63: by the addition of hundreds, &c. you increase 09 to 2509, which multiplied by 7 gives the proposed sum. Is 2,509 a prime number? consult the table for 09; after the previous examinations you come to 13, which multiplied by 93, gives 1209; increase it 13x193= 2509; therefore 13x7=91, which multiplied by 193, will give another pair of factors. Is 193 a prime number? it will be found such; therefore 7x2509, and 91x193, are the only factors. It may be borne in mind, as an universal rule, that when a simple number will not prove itself a factor, any other number compounded of that simple one will not; for instance, 21 is formed by 3x7; if 3 or 7 does hot divide the number sought, neither will 21. And also in high numbers, after the right hand figures have been increased by the addition of hundreds and thousands, the left hand figures may be increased in the same manner. It is necessarily a slow process, though a sure one. Again, it is not necessary to continue the operation by trying numbers that are above the nearest square root to the sum proposed.

OS CO

No notice is taken in this table of the terminations of even number; for they may be divided by two, four, &c. nor yet of 5, as an ending figure for 5 will always divide itself.

RULE OF MULTIPLICATION.

This method was made known at Birmingham, in the Spring of 1816; its peculiarity consists in beginning at the left hand, disposing first of the higher numerals, then the next highest; and so on to the end.

Example.

What is the product of 4791x238? Divide the two terms thus:—4000 700 200 90 30

1 8

True, the method here exhibited requires a much larger number of figures than the common Rule, but it will be remembered that pen, ink and paper, cost Zerah very little, when engaged in a sum. It is thought that the present mode has decided advantage over any other that is known, for such as wish to reckon in the head. The large numbers found first are easily retained, because consisting of so many ciphers; he describes the steps that the rule involves; his own mind was enabled to take these steps and hurry on to the result, not indeed quicker than thought, but more rapidly than his eye could have glanced at the figures they contain.

A FEW PIECES IN RHYME.

The following little pieces were written in the days of boyhood; they are not inserted to claim any merit on the score of poetical talent, but rather to give a more full idea of the subject of this memoir in other things than arithmetic. —If they are worthy of criticism, he is glad to be instructed, though since he engaged in ministerial duties, he has had no time or taste for composition of this kind.

THE EXILE. In festive hall the sprightly dancers bound,

And move, obedient to the harper's sound;

Youth's mirthful revels cheer the noon of night,

And age's cheek reflects a gladsome light.

Far from the train, on tissued couch reclined,

Mark ye yon lone one, who no joy can find

Observe that brow by many a line defaced;

His country's exile, by dishonor chased;

Ambition's votary in his youthful prime;

Now driven, unfriended, from his native clime.

Behold that eye, once filled with ardent flame;

By legions followed as the star of Fame.

That heaving bosom, seat of rising hope:

Now prey to thoughts with which it cannot cope;

The sigh suppressed; the check'd, yet starting tear;

And should by chance some strain salute his ear,

Once heard with rapture in his native vale,

Before in blasted youth, his spirit fell,

. In agonizing hues his thought portrays-Scenes as delightful in his early days.

And more distressing yet! blithe as this train,

His children once pressed light their native plain.

Now, maddening thought! from sire's embraces torn,

Far from their mother's cell, o'er billows borne.

For him, no duteous hands his pain assuage,

Or smooth the piUow of declining age.

What hopes in store for him? No wonder then

If sighs, if bursting tears disclose his pain.

The herdsman's axe, the battle's ruthless yell,

The fated lightning, or the watery swell,

Were more, more welcome far, for who would roam

O'er foreign lands, to seek a peaceful tomb *I*

In bitter hopelessness of soul would rove,

His life uncheered by wife's or children's love,

His day illumed by no enlivening sun,

To light his passage to the blest Unknown.

JUNE 16, 1815.

On yonder hill, with lofty oaks bedeckt, Whose spreading boughs throw o'er the barren soil A sombre shade, on that ill-fated morn, Napoleon stood. Ask not to know how he Had armed his heart with hopes—how he had manned The wakeful fancies in his breast against The adverse fortune of unequal fight. Once more he ruled supreme.—An Empire's flower Rode in his eager vanguard, every breast Anxious for battle—prompt to dye their swords In hostile gore—and hence extending far To right, to left, in numerous files moved on The hope, the bulwark of an Emperor's pride, Sons, husbands, fathers; some with ruthless hastt The trumpet's clangor from a fair one's arms With brazen throat divided. They obeyed, All swift to guard the sovereign of their choice. He on his milk-white steed, with swelling heart Surveys the field, and leads his searching eye Upon each rank; explores the adverse host, Ai the bright sun casts on their polished arms On this day commenced the battle of Waterleo.

His cloud emerging beams—he notes the fire That lights Ins liegemen's eyes, and gladly hails la them the certain omens of success.

MAY 5, 1821.

Wmip, Gallia's sons, who oft at glory's call, Followed Napoleon to the field of fame!

Weep, high-souled matrons, who in bannered hall,

Have fired your children's breasts to deeds of flame! How oft, contemning ease inglorious, rushed, Onward by war's shrill trumpet's echo led,

The hope of France, with youthful ardor flushed,

To well earned victory or a soldier's bed!

This day their chief, who hurled his lightnings round

From Gallia's fields to Europe's farthest vale— Their chief, who heard so oft glad triumph's sound

In lively measures swell the morning gale, Died captive—on a rock 'mid ocean's wave,

Shut out forever from the joys of life, Did Europe's terror once, now find a grave,

So long denied him in the crimson strife., A tender wife torn from his aching breast; A cherished son to distant regions borne;

Those men who round his prosperous eagle pressed,

All vanished, fleeting as the hues of morn.

His soul, indignant at her crying wrongs,

Formed great by Nature, daring, proud, and free, So long the mark of slander's hundred tongues,

Impatient burst from thrall to liberty!

FRIENDSHIP.

Thb rose will droop when wintry blasts prevail,

And perish, stricken by the chilling gale;

But on that gale, though lost its summer bloom,

Is borne on balmy wing, its soft perfume.

So Friendship, sacred bond! one radiant gleam

That cheers our sojourn on this earthly frame,

When reckless hands dissolve its flowery chain,

Too often never may revive again.

Perhaps the memory of the days gone by

In some fond breast may wake an anxious sigh;

The wish, that gentler touch had grasped the tie,

That linked two bosoms in firm amity.

While pride, that soul of man, from angels sprung,

Which recreant those from heavenly splendors flung,

Unbending spirit! teaches to disdain

Submission to the One who broke the chain.

The dawn of youth—the hope of better days,

May fire the soul, and tune the poet's lays;

Faded and gone—what pleasure can remain

To cheer his passage through this world of pain?

Youth's first affections vanish and decay;

Life's brightest dreams on fleeting pinions stray;

And thou, fond man, where is thy joyous hour?

Lone 'mid thy visioned bliss thou stand'st a blighted flower.

THE LAND OF MY BIRTH.

'tjs the land of my birth!' tis the land of my sires,

Where the standard of Freedom serenely shall wave, While virtue shall quicken with gathering fires, And lead on to battle the strong and the brave!

Though invaders may lower, and tyranny threaten

To cast her dark shadow o'er Freedom's domain,

Their valor shall lead them 'gainst Gaul and 'gainst Britain,

Nor shall liberty quail to the lords of the main!

Unfading thy memory! though distant thy beacons,

And far over ocean beams thy setting sun, Thy genius inspires me, and powerfully wakens

Remembrance of deeds for our liberties done.

When pride and ambition, like two mountain streams rushing,

Would o'erwhelm the wide earth in their ravaging sway, Though many have fallen, yet while life's streams were gushing,

Their spirits beamed forth as the radiance of day! How joyful they fell! and yielding life's fountains,

In purple tides streaming from bravely earned death, Their last dying gaze fixed on their loved mountains,

These words, high exulting, exhausted their breath: "For the land of my birth! for the land of my sires!

Where the standard of Freedom serenely shall wave, While virtue shall quicken with gathering fires,

And lead on to battle, the strong and the brave!'" ETERNITY.

Eternity? say what is that *l* what

amazing quality of created time can secure its existence longer than mortal thought can reach *l* The life of man, by some esteemed so long a period, is as a breath; the annals of nations from age to age, would make no chasm in the boundless chain, being lost. Yes, thousands of years from hence, when I shall have mouldered into dust; when all the peopled earth shall have changed her numerous lords more than a thousand times; when all the busy vanities of life will be no more remembered by us, He shall exist. From the dawn of new creation, from the morning when His eye shone o'er the wild of the waters; millions of centuries ere those waters floated o'er the incrusted earth—until time, and period, and history, shall have passed away, His reign will but begin. More boundless than yon lucid fields of space, the time gone by, will to the future seem less, far less, than the smallest particle of sand upon the Atlantic shore to this globe, to all the assembled spheres of heaven, close upon the centre piled.

TRANSLATED FROM THE LATIN.

Like the dim moon which lights the dusky evej

And bids our labors cease, is Nature's ray;

But grace celestial which our souls receive,

Beams brighter than the radiant orb of day.

LINES ADDRESSED TO REV., FITZWILLIAM,

N. H. 1624.

He is returned—yea—from a distant clime;

His youthful brow as yet unscathed by time;

The aspiring hopes, the fire of youthful blood

This day high soaring, and the next subdued.

O'er fairest prospects in life's genial spring,

Full oft has desolation spread her wing.

When friendship's song has cheered his arduous way

Even long enough to bid him hope the day

Of suffering past, her altered note has shown,

The syren's voice led on to rocks unknown,

Where hope was shipwrecked—all escape were vain,

"Submit and suffer, for 'tis misery's reign."

Now fairer prospects may allure to rise,

Lord of his fate—ah no—its mysteries

No mortal ken may trace—perchance indeed

If once explored, 'twere safer far to read

An awful summons to another world,

Mid rolling thunders and the lightnings hurled.

Thou, who wouldstof him learn, and numbers more,

Who speak full kindly on our western shore,

He has no griefs to soothe—they are his own,

Nor ask the consolation even of one,

Remote from those whose friendship cheered his hours,

When joy raised high, or sorrow quelled his powers.

He hopes, nor fears in duty's path to move,

Alone seems hard, requires aid—from above.

He feels himself a debtor—more than thee

Have claims upon him, and he would be free.

He would not ask the sympathy of one—

Nor would he scorn that sympathy once shown.

Farewell! may brighter, days to these succeed,

And happier prospects be thy children's meed.

INVITATION.

Deeds of praise are unavailing, All our idle works are dead,

His the glory of fulfilling

That emprize for which he bled.

Songs of triumph, loudly ringing,

Should his boundless love proclaim:

Hear the choirs of angels singing

Loud hosannas to his name.

In the courts of love immortal,

Harps celestial sound his praise;

Now, even now, heaven's highest portal

Echoes back the hallowed lays.

Mortals come! with reverence bending

Round the footsteps of his throne;

Now embrace the wide extending

Full atonement of his Son.

ADDRESSED TO A MISSIONARY.

Yea strive with toil and hunger; firmly stand, And meet the fleeting troubles of thy way; Move on supported by that powerful hand Who guides His people to the realms of day. What though thou meetest the blast, the wintry shower, The mortal woes that make our nature start; Though suffering cross thy steps in every hour; Disease and anguish bear their equal part; Yet dost thou fear? Canst doubt His mighty arm, Whose mandate quiets restless nature's breast; Who speaks in thunder, and who walks the storm; Who ever blesses and is ever blest? In happier climes thy wayward lot is cast; 'Neath brighter suns is filed thy cairn abode;

Yea, soon the confines of this world are past,

And thou a seraph near the throne of God.

THE SABBATH.

Hie to the temples of our Lord and King,

And bring Him honors worthy of His name;

Stand up, ye saints inspired with hallowed flame; To Heaven's eternal One loud anthems sing. This day is His,—'tis consecrate to Him,

Whose Sabbath told creation's work was done;

On this day genial rose the golden sun. Rejoicing, round he throws his kindling beam.

The waves of ocean sink in soft repose;

The northern tempest calls his terrors home;

The south wind gently sways the empyreal dome; On violets breathing, fragrance round him throws. In his deep cavern rests the lion's pride;

The eagle's war-cry rings not through the heaven;

By lightning's path no bedded rock

is riven; A day of rest was named—of rest, the world replied. To Thee, our Father, bounteous Lord and King,

Whose love paternal stays our feeble years; Whose truth supports us, stills our rising fears,

A song of praise immortal would we sing.

Do Thou inspire us, guide our wayward feet;

And while we praise Thee, let us not offend;

Oh be Thou near us till our lives shall end, Then give us mansions near thy blissful seat.

SPRING.

Y«s spring returns. Another winter'past,

The gloomy season o'er, once more returns

The seed time of the year. Of our short year

When will the seed time come? Still move we on;

The rose now budding blossoms, full blo-wndies—

The green herb shoots its lance above the sod,

Suns genial smile; its hour at length is come.

Ko warning given, it falls. Where is its pride J

So we, dull, lifeless race! shame can it be,

Senseless as native earth 1 Aye, truly, earth—

How well we prove our origin. The dust Upon yon hill might claim its rank with us.

Oh who can slight the calls of nature's God

From his high palace in the upper heavens

More haughtily than we? Young, happy, fair,

Pride of our friends, gazed on by wondering eyes,

And ever seeking, where we may best gain

Small meed of praise for some even smaller act,

And fix the fool's regard upon our path,

While to the cries, the warning voice of Heaven,

The calls of Mercy and the menaced

wrath
Blindly we turn a calm and careless ear.
When is our seed time? When our
spring of days?
Now is the seed time—weed well our
little spot
With care watch o'er it—heed not
storms. No blight
(We have his promise) shall assail our
charge,
And when mature and ripe, our Hus-
bandman
Will purge the harvest from each little
mote
And give us mansions in the seats of
light.

WHERE IS BEAUTY?

Who seeks for Beauty? Who would
gaze upon
Perfection limitless and teach his soul
New songs of rapture? Shall he bend
on woman
His ardent eye? Though fair she per-
ishes.
Nature's gay countenance, when
Spring returns,
May cheer his soul and tune the vocal
lay;
It perishes. Who seeks such frail
memorial
Of God's beneficence? Shall man,
adorned
With reason? Can no higher holier
theme
Inspire his soul? O, if in Heaven can
be
Beauty's perfection, it was when ar-
rayed
In mercy, dearest of His attributes,
Messiah left his seats of happiness.
O, who can paint the new-born glory
shining,
Upon God's brow, when through the
yielding air
He sought our Planet. Though he
came alone,
Millions were round him, with him.
Could their praise
Add to his glory? Could the universe
Through all her boundless fields of
radiance pour
Even one hosanna to enhance his
bliss?
When man would teach his tongue
immortal lays,

To speak the glories of the coming
Christ,
He feels his weakness, if he views
aright
Transcendant love—yea, love in all
its beauty.
He cannot paint it. Thou hast seen a
mother
Anxiously watching her first-born on
his bed
Of languishing—yea, thou hast heard
her sigh,
As dire disease advanced to seize his
prey;
Or heard how once the lion from his
den
Escaping, yielded to a mother's
prayers
Her darling lost. Such things are
common now;
Both can perform an act of love, of
kindness.
But that the Majesty of power, ar-
rayed
In love, should to the proudest enemy,
Adulterers, murderers, blasphemy's
first-born,
Liars, and—sinners—let one word
express it—
Say, "Live! accept my righteousness
and live.
Break off your sins, and to yon bleed-
ing cross
Where I, your ransom, shall anon be
nailed,
Bring your repentant souls, dearer to
me
Than heavenly radiance." We can
meditate,
And so we ought. We may, we must
believe.
No more is needed. Who could com-
prehend?

TO A BEREAVED MOTHER.

Oh canst thou weep, while bending o'er
her form,
Thy tender blossom nipp'd so early
dead?
Refrain thy transports. Check thy
soul's alarm,
Nor think an enemy this shaft has sped.
It ia recorded that in the city ol
Florence, a linn escaped from his cage,
and rushing out of the streets-a general

panic ensued. A woman in her flight,
let tier infant fall. Turning round she
saw him in the lion's fangs, and rushing
she fell on her knees before him. The
king of beasts-as if overpowered by ma-
ternal lore, gave up the child unhurt,
and quietly submitted to baled back by
hiskecper.

A mother's love embalms her cold remains.

True she is gone—but where? Sure
thou hast thought, 'Tis dear to memory
to recal fond scenes
Of happiness. Are they too dearly
bought?
She rests in peace. Affection may recal
Her nameless charms of youth. Those
charms were given Not to ensnare thy
heart—so dear to all,
But gain her mansions in the courts of
Heaven.

OCCASIONAL PROLOGUE FOR GUSTAVUS
VASA, PER-

FORMED BY THE STUDENTS OF FAIR-
FIELD ACAD-

EMY.

The Historic muse, extending through
all time
Her eye, far darting o'er each distant
clime,
To-night records the valorous deeds of
one,
"Who hurled Ambition from her lofty
throne.
When suffering sires, and injured
daughters wept,
And heaven-born Justice lay enthralled,
not slept,
He dared alone through Sweden's
mountains wave,
Woe to the tyrant! his unconquered
glaive.
He fought and vanquished,—burst each
slavish band
That long in fetters bound his native
land.
A strain of Glory, e'en though feebly
sung,
Her thrilling chords e'en though but
weakly strung,
Is echoed back from every breast of
flame,
And sounds immortal from the
awak'ning theme.

When Freedom's haughty son disdains to grace
The pride of him who tramples on his race—
When martial ardor fires each mountain child,
And all stand forth to guard their native wild,
Dearer than glimpse of day to dungeoned slave,
Than manacles are hateful to the brave,
What bosom beats not? Say, who does not feel
His heart exulting high with rapture swell.
On such a scene to-night we fix our eyes,
Nor scom our efforts. Oh, do not despise
If in green youth, by Nature schooled alone,
We seek approval. While on Denmark's throne
One of our number sits, oh do not scan
If skilled or not, he rules his little band;
And as Gustavus treads the mimic war,
Be censure loud and secret whisper far.
With mildness contemplate our new career,
The statesman's error, and the lover's fear.
"With mildness view whatever may offend;
Another scene may see more sweetly blend
Touches of Nature with our untaught rage,
And lays far worthier of a Fairfield Stage.

TO A LADY ON REMOVING WITH HER FAMILY TO A DISTANT HOME.

The day at length is come. Thou bidst farewell To these green hills where passed thy infant years,
O'er whose tall summits wintry tempests swell,
And Spring first smiles, like Beauty in her tears.
Perchance where happier fields their blossoms bear,
More genial climes their milder influence shed,
The smiles of Fortune, when she seems most fair,
May banish memory of our mountain's shade.
Oh no, it cannot. Onward roll the stream
Of chequer'd life; still varying be the road;
Thou'lt still remember, as an ancient dream,
Delightful scenes where once thy footsteps trod;
The fond endearments of a parent's love:—
Thou art a parent. Shall thy babes forget,
If haply distant from thy side they rove,
Her tender care, who made all suffering sweet?
I hear thee sigh; I mark the gushing tear
That speaks the anguish of thy sad farewell;
Until this hour, thou little knew'st how dear,
How valued friends, contained thy native dell.
Yet shall ye meet again. No, Sorrow cries;
But Hope, exulting, shall the scene renew;
Gay Hope shall cheer thee, bid new prospects rise,
And future pleasures fill thy raptured view.
All good be thine. While life's glad currents run,
May rich enjoyments cheer thy grateful heart;
Affliction may reward thy duty done,
But shall a Christian sink beneath her dart?
Where is thy hope? on him who traced this lay?
Vain hope—thy dearest friends? they are but dust.
Upon what earthly power so fleeting? nay—
Be it on him who shall reward the just.

LINES WRITTEN FOR THE FIRST OF JANUARY, 1826.

Tis buried with the thousand witnesses
That round Jehovah's throne shall testify
Of righteousness or sin. Yes, Adam's race,
Look back and tiink, long years are swallowed up;
Years that have seen thy childhood's playful hours,
Thy youthful dreams of happiness and love,
The blighted hopes, the sorrows of thy prime.
Where are they gone? What will they speak of thee 7
My brother, do they point thee to the day
When thou shalt stand before the blazing throne,
And see thy risen Saviour and thy God?
When Earth's confusion shakes the roofless sky,
When Nature's ruin tells Uie judgment near,
Will Faith's bright shield protect thy trembling head J
Here yawn the opening graves: the rising dead
Come forth in strange array: new bodies greet
The anxious eye: to some, Jehovah calls,
"Come near, ye blessed! here are seats prepared
For such as you from new creation's birth:"
Others shall hear words of more awful sound,
"Cursed, avaunt! there see the livid flames,
The grisly demons of the dark abyss,
That greedy wait to seize their destined prey."
Canst thou in patience gaze upon the wreck,
Nor ask "Is this my portion, this the place
Where I must groan a long eternity?"
Or do they bid thy sweet remembrance turn
To that prized moment when thy heart received
The witness of the Spirit that thou wert
Embraced in full communion with thy God,
The Father, Son, and Holy Comforter!
I hope they do. Happy art thou, my brother.
But must they speak of years forgotten now,

Spent in the service of this fickle world,
Its false alluring vanities? Oh, think!
Can such a retrospect support a soul
Declared immortal by her Maker's voice?
Hast thou resolved to serve and be destroyed
By that most fell and miserable fiend,
Who wants companions in his lowest hell?
Rouse up, for shame! look where the Saviour died
Where bursting rocks and opening sepulchres

Told that Redemption was accomplished now.
He groaned for you and me—for all mankind.
And were it not full mournful that a soul
Should not be saved, after such vast display,
Such Fountains opened for Jerusalem?
Come forth, my brother, to the lowly cross!
He bore it; will not thou? I trust thou wilt.
Let the destroyer's realm be shaken from
Its broad foundations. Be thy Captain, Christ;
Thy breastplate Righteousness, thy helmet bright
Salvation full and free. Though thunders roll,
Though blasts may sweep thee, 'twill but help thee on
To seats of glory far beyond the grave,
To seats of happiness from sorrow free.

CPSIA information can be obtained at www.ICGtesting.com
Printed in the USA
LVOW112132030412

276063LV00004B/24/P

9 781151 291851